GUIDE TO

DOGS

SIMON WHALEY

© Haynes Publishing 2018
Published June 2018

A CIP Catalogue record for this book
is available from the British Library.

ISBN: 978 1 78521 243 7

Library of Congress control no. 2018932890

Published by Haynes Publishing,
Sparkford, Yeovil, Somerset BA22 7JJ
Tel: 01963 440635
Int. tel: +44 1963 440635
Website: www.haynes.com

Printed in Malaysia.

Bluffer's Guide®, Bluffer's® and Bluff Your Way®
are registered trademarks.

Series Editor: David Allsop.
Front cover illustration by Alan Capel.

CONTENTS

It's a Dog's Life   5

The Biggest Bluff of All   9

A Breed Apart   17

Give a Dog a Bad Name   25

Canine Characteristics   33

Dinner Time   43

Puppy Power   51

Health and Safety   61

Fun and Games   69

On the Job   85

Memorable Mutts   97

Pooch Poetry   107

Man's (and Woman's) Best Friend   115

Glossary   121

— ℬ —

*'The one absolutely unselfish
friend that man can have... the one that
never deserts him and the
one that never proves ungrateful
or treacherous is his dog...'*

George Graham Vest

IT'S A DOG'S LIFE

It is a truth universally acknowledged that a human in possession of a good home must be in want of a dog… especially because of the huge prize money available from entering them into TV talent shows.

However, in a world where fame lasts no longer than 15 seconds (a relatively long time in dog years), it may come as a surprise to discover that the domestic dog (*Canis lupus familiaris*) and mankind (*Homo sapiens*) have been working together for over 15,000 years, making it one of the most successful inter-species relationships in history. The irony is not lost on the astute dog bluffer who will have spotted that, when many of man's own relationships break down, more effort is put into fighting for custody of the dog than anything else except the children (and sometimes even them).

The most famous description of the bond between man and dog can be attributed to an American politician and lawyer, George Graham Vest. In September 1870, he represented a dog owner whose faithful four-legged companion, Old Drum, had been shot dead by a local sheep farmer. This farmer had publicly declared that any dog found on his property would be shot. Old Drum's owner sued for damages, and, in a classic courtroom drama, Vest turned to the jury and said: 'The one absolutely unselfish friend that man can have … the one that never deserts him and the one that never proves ungrateful or treacherous is his dog…He guards the sleep of his pauper master as if he were a prince. When all other friends desert, he remains.'

Vest's heartfelt words pulled the jury's heartstrings so strongly that he won the case, and Old Drum's owner was awarded $500 compensation (so the story goes), 10 times the maximum limit for damages at that time. Since that day, dogs have been known as man's best friend.

Many millions of dog owners since have happily invited their canine friends into their homes, spending hours training them to sit, stay, and roll over dead when they shout 'bang' at them. You will of course realise that in these dog-friendly households it is the dog who has successfully trained the family to run around after him or her, not the other way around.

But dogs are social animals. Leave them home alone for too long and they might be tempted to trash the place. Alternatively, they'll simply leave something unpleasant in your bed, chew the chair legs on your dining furniture, and annoy the neighbours with their incessant howling. Dog-behaviour specialists refer to this as 'separation anxiety'. Dog owners refer to it as bloody annoying. How else are they supposed to pay the vet bills if they don't go out to work? It's a fair enough point, but if they can't make arrangements for the dog to be walked in their absence, they might wonder about the wisdom of having a dog in the first place. Very few dogs' homes and rescue centres will rehome a dog unless there are guarantees about regular daily routines involving plenty of exercise and activity. And then there's the dog to consider.

Dogs can be the ideal companion for many people: they don't answer back (apart from a warning growl if you try to detach them from a chew), they don't care if you leave the seat up on the toilet (in fact, this often makes drinking out of the toilet bowl easier for them) and they're more than happy to curl up on the sofa with you and watch a football game or a soppy film. However, in younger families with nearly every member at school or work, there's often little for the dog to do on their own during the day. There's only so much daytime TV any dog can take. So if you want be taken seriously as somebody who understands something of the particular group dynamics involved in a situation where a human family and a dog live together, then you will need a grasp of the essential facts – which is where this short guide can help you.

This book sets out to conduct you through the main danger zones encountered in discussions about dogs, and to equip you with a vocabulary and evasive technique that will minimise the risk of being rumbled as a bluffer. It will give you a few easy-to-learn hints and methods that might even allow you to be accepted as a dog expert of rare knowledge and experience. But it will do more. It will give you the tools to impress legions of marvelling listeners with your wisdom and insight – without anyone discovering that until you read it you probably didn't know the difference between a pekapoo and a shih-tzu.

When it jumps onto a double bed, a dog will seek to split the human occupants by lying down between them, gradually nudging them further apart. It will rarely be satisfied until at least one of you is on the floor.

THE BIGGEST BLUFF
OF ALL

A dog is not a wolf in sheep's clothing (otherwise it would look like a sheep). However, today's domestic dogs do share a significant amount of DNA with their wolf cousins. There is a debate about when the relationship between man and wolf, or dog, first began to develop; some say it was 14,000 years ago, while others say it could be as many as 17,000 years ago. The bluffer does not need to split dog hairs over this. Suffice to say that scientists are using fossils to determine this information, so however you look at it, it was a very long time ago.

With all relationships, it takes two to tango, and in this most unusual relationship (for the dog is the only species to take instructions from another animal species as if it were its own), it was the dog who tangoed the first step. Proof, if ever any more were needed, that dogs have been training humans for far longer than humans think they've been training dogs.

Initially, wolves were attracted to man because of the fire he had created to keep himself warm. This vestigial link continues today, with most dogs successfully curling up in front of the domestic fire, preventing much of the heat reaching the human.

HUNTING HOUNDS

Like humans, dogs are hunters. However, they're also opportunists. If a human is stupid enough to leave an unattended joint of meat at nose height on a kitchen worktop, a dog is not going to examine its conscience and turn down the opportunity to eat it. They are intelligent animals, who were quick to realise that while they had the means to hunt in packs and bring down huge beasts, there were easier ways of finding supper. Scavenging for food is much safer. Why go out and risk being seriously harmed in the hunt for food, when you can send a human to get a tin of something chunky in gravy from the nearest supermarket?

Despite what many bluffers might think, Stone Age man was quite civilised. For example, while he had yet to discover the delights of supermarket loyalty cards, he had adopted a system of throwing food scraps into one big pile outside of the main settlement area. This meant that rats and other vermin were kept at bay. It appears even Stone Age man had problems getting the local council to come along and empty the bins on a fortnightly basis. Wolves began making the most of this free food opportunity and soon realised it was worth keeping in favour with the human species.

TERRITORIAL TENDENCIES

In addition to sharing the hunting instinct, wolves and humans realised they had something else in common: they were territorial. Now that wolves had found this useful source of food, they protected it from other dangerous animals hoping to tuck into a free lunch. Whenever another hungry, slavering beast got too close to the cave or encampment, the wolves would bark and howl, alerting the humans to the potential danger. Together, they saw off many threats, and it was through this cooperation that man and wolf began cohabiting. By pretending that the human was the dominant partner, the wolf laid the foundations of a convincing bluff that no other non-human species has since surpassed.

THE FAMILY CANIDAE

There are many subspecies within the canine world (dogs, wolves, jackals, dingoes, foxes and coyotes), but they all belong to the biological family known as *Canidae*. DNA evidence suggests the first canines to be domesticated were grey wolves (*Canis lupus*). These were social animals who, after mating for life, often travelled around in family groups, only looking for a new partner when their current partner had died, or been killed. Clearly, they had lots to teach humans about loyalty and fidelity.

The size of a wolf family pack will range from 5 and 12 animals, with the parent wolves – the alpha male and alpha female – at the core, and an elaborate hierarchy of offspring of various ages below them. When the younger wolves become sexually mature, they tend to go off and look for a mate and create their own pack. Many people might feel a profound admiration for an animal species where the kids actually fly the nest and don't return on a Sunday afternoon three or four years later, broke and with two months' worth of washing in a collection of bin bags.

A wolf is a predatory animal, often tracking prey over large distances. Its cunning allows it to remain hidden for as long as possible, and when the intended victim finally realises how close it is to meeting its maker, its reaction can determine whether it lives or dies. Wolves enjoy the chase. If their prey stands its ground, a wolf may give up and ignore it. But if the wolves fancy a little fun, they'll try to spook it into running.

If you achieve nothing else in training your dog, ban it from sleeping on your bed. Otherwise, very soon it will be sleeping in it and you'll be on the dog blanket.

If they chase a group of animals, wolves will attempt to split the group, and then home in on one particular member of it. With their prey in sight, they'll try to force it over rougher ground to slow it down, or corner it at a dead end or sheer drop. An observant bluffer might notice that the family dog adopts similar tactics. When it jumps onto a double bed, a dog will seek to split the human occupants by lying down between them, gradually nudging them further apart. It will rarely be satisfied until at least one of you is on the floor. There is a vital lesson to be learnt here. If you achieve nothing else in training your dog, ban it from sleeping on your bed. Otherwise, very soon it will be sleeping in it and you'll be on the dog blanket. This is known as alpha dog syndrome. Other signs include:

- The best seat in the living room belongs to the dog. It's the one nearest the fire and with the best view of the TV. In extreme cases the remote control is Velcroed to the armrest.

- The dog sits at the head of the table at dinner time.

- The dog is the first one to leave the house when the family pack goes out as a group, and is also the first one to enter on their return.

- When the family pack goes out in the car, the dog travels in the front passenger seat.

- On walks, the dog will be the first through gates and over stiles. It will always be ahead of the leading human in the group.

Dogs that are true domestic pets (or animal companions as we must learn to call them in these PC times) tend to be the ones who succeed in dominating their pack. Dogs trained to undertake specific jobs as part of the human-canine team, such as sheep dogs, police dogs or guide dogs, are trained to know their place from the moment they join the human pack. However, non-dog-owning bluffers may take the attitude that all dogs are alpha dogs. After all, in the human-dog relationship, who's the one who goes round picking up whose poop? If you were a visiting Martian, who would you think was in charge?

FROM WOLF TO DOG

Turning a wolf into a dog was not a trick Stone Age man managed to pull off overnight. It took many successive generations of wolves and humans to finally negotiate the deal that would lead to wolves agreeing to be fed, sheltered and kept warm in return for helping with the hunting and gathering, and warning of an unexpected visitor at the cave door.

Modern-day experiments to domesticate wolves have failed. Wolf pups can be hand-reared and are quite tame, but by the time they reach maturity, their wolf DNA has kicked in and told them that there is an alternative to human society. A dog might know not to bite the hand that feeds it, but researchers soon discovered that a wolf isn't quite so respectful, especially if the hand doing the feeding looks more appetising than the dried dog food being offered as an alternative.

The wolves that survived were the ones who learned to live side by side with humans – without biting them. Any scavenging wolf that posed a threat to our ancestors was summarily sent packing. Therefore, only the wolves with gentler temperaments were invited over the doorstep. 'Two Socks' in the 1990 film *Dances With Wolves* is a good example of a wolf with the right sort of attitude.

Scientists have realised that today's dogs, even when fully grown and mature, still exhibit many puppy-like qualities. Whereas a wolf pup is happy to frolic about with a ball, a fully grown wolf isn't. One of the major differences between adult wolves and adult dogs is that adult dogs still retain a playful attitude and juvenile qualities. The technical term, should you need to drop this into a conversation with a dog owner is 'neoteny': the retention of child-like features in an adult. Many women often use this term about husbands and boyfriends who have a knack of regressing to their four-year-old selves when their football team loses.

Indeed, should you find yourself being asked the question: what's the difference between a wolf and a dog? You can confidently answer 1.8%. That's the only difference between a wolf's DNA and a dog's DNA. Domestic dogs are essentially wolf puppies that have grown up physically, but not reached emotional maturity. That's why many women prepare for life with a man by first practising with a dog.

Any dog loves its owner unconditionally, no matter what its ancestry. As any fellow bluffer will tell you; it's not where you're from that's important, but who you have running around after you.

A BREED APART

CREATING DIFFERENT BREEDS

Although the grey wolf may have been the first canine to be domesticated, it wasn't the only dog-like animal humans were experimenting with. As well as jackals and coyotes, whose genes have been utilised in breeding good working dogs, even the distinctly dodgy dingo is said to have been involved in the genetic history of the good-natured, loyal and devoted Australian sheepdog known as a 'kelpie'.

Since man and dog came together, the relationship has mainly been one of mutual respect and reliance. Man would look after the dog's basic needs if the dog earned its keep by working for him. Through the ages man and dog have evolved together. When the former began cultivating crops he needed the latter to keep vermin at bay. Small dogs were better at this because they could chase rats down holes and tunnels. When man discovered how to farm animals in the same way as crops he soon realised that his dog could be used to herd animals, such as sheep and goats. Bigger, but more agile dogs were better at keeping these animals on their hooves. And when he began building castles and palaces he knew he needed even bigger, fiercer-looking dogs to guard the gates and drawbridges. As the saying goes, you don't keep a dog and bark yourself – unless you're a newspaper editor/proprietor, a football manager, or a drill sergeant in the army.

The benefit of dogs having family trees is that it provides something else for them to cock their legs up against.

As time progressed, man realised that certain breeds had specific qualities and that if he needed a dog that was small but plucky and determined he needed to find parents with each of these qualities. For some characteristics this was a bit hit and miss, but eventually our ancestors figured out that if you keep mixing the right genes together you should end up with the qualities you're looking for, and a new breed of dog is born. It's the same for humans too, although it's called eugenics, practised unwittingly by Scandinavian peoples for centuries until it was given a bad name by the Nazis.

There are three main breed classifications that bluffers should be aware of, so as not to inadvertently offend a dog's owner. (You'll never inadvertently offend the dog; they'll always be pleased to see you.) They are:

Pedigree A pedigree dog is a pure-bred dog whose parents are both of the same breed, as are all of their ancestors, traceable all the way back to the establishment of their breed. It's like humans having ancestry that you can trace back to William the Conqueror. The benefit of dogs having family trees is that it provides something else for them to cock their legs up against.

Crossbreed A crossbreed dog is not a mongrel. There is a huge difference, as any owner of a crossbreed will quickly point out. Both parents of a crossbreed dog are pedigree animals, although they are not of the same breed. In human terms, it's like an heir to a Scottish ancestral dynasty marrying into an English ancestral dynasty. This, of course, has been happening for centuries, mostly successfully as today's Royal Family proves (except in that instance it involved a Scottish/German/Greek dynasty).

Mongrel A mongrel dog is the result of having beer-goggle eyes on a Friday or Saturday night and then waking up the following morning, still unsure who or what you've slept with. Mongrel dogs are the result of random breeding where the parents are of mixed ancestry too. Each one is unique.

Bluffers who may be thinking of acquiring a new puppy for their own home should be aware of each of these three categories – not because of the differences in characteristics and temperaments, but because of the damage each will have on your finances. A pedigree puppy could cost thousands, a crossbreed might fetch half the price, whereas an entire pack of mongrels can be picked up for nothing. Talk to any true dog owner though and they'll tell you it doesn't matter. Any dog loves its owner unconditionally, no matter what its ancestry. As any fellow bluffer will tell you; it's not where you're from that's important, but who you have running around after you.

DESIGNER DOGS

While crossbreeding has the benefit of creating dogs with useful abilities and character attributes, the media has labelled some of these as designer or 'boutique' dogs. This is because when bred together, the results invariably have humorous portmanteau names. Bring together a Labrador and a poodle and the hybrid offspring will be known as a 'labradoodle'. If one parent is a cocker spaniel and the other is a poodle, all puppies are known as 'cockapoos'. Should a Pekingese and a poodle mate the result is a 'pekapoo', and if ever a shih-tzu and a poodle were to get amorous, their offspring would be a rather unromantic 'shihtpoo'. Unsurprisingly shih-tzus are very popular with those hybrid breeders of a scatological bent, especially if a small energetic terrier known as a Jack Russell is involved. Not that most of us give a Jack shiht.

CANINE CLASSIFICATIONS

Having bred our dogs to fulfil certain working requirements, it was only logical that we devised a classification system based on their specific skills. A basic knowledge of these different breeds will assist in how you react to them, should you find yourself cornered by one.

Gun dog/Sporting

These dogs were bred for their agility and high-energy levels, making them perfect for collecting game shot by their owners. When pheasants and other game birds are blasted out of the sky, a faithful gun dog will bound across the countryside to retrieve the carcass. If the hapless creature is still twitching, the gun dog will swiftly 'despatch it' with a vigorous shake of the head. Most importantly he will not tear it apart. That pleasure is reserved for his human master, or their manservant/cook.

Popular gun dog breeds include: Retrievers (the clue is in the name), both golden and Labrador; spaniels such as the cocker and English springer; and setters, like the English, Irish and red.

Hounds

While a gun dog will retrieve your kill once you've comprehensively perforated it with buckshot, a hound will help you locate your prey in the first place. Dogs that track by sight or smell fall into this category, and are generally quite laid back in temperament, making them ideal family pets. They can be easily distracted, especially if they come across a more intriguing scent than the one they're supposed to follow. This can include a wide range of vermin, roadkill, raptor kill, cats and other dogs. You might think they're following the scent of a game bird, but don't be surprised if you find yourself aiming at the rotting carcass of a hapless victim of something higher up the food chain.

Common hounds include: bassets and beagles, who do all of the sniffing, and the greyhounds, whippets and Afghan hounds that hunt by sight.

Pastoral

Parents with lots of children like pastoral dogs because they're great for rounding up the kids and stopping them from wandering off. Used mainly by farmers and stock herdsmen, one dog can control hundreds of sheep. These sheepdogs are highly intelligent animals, capable of coping with lots of stimulation (so counting sheep doesn't send them to sleep). They have so much energy that they refuse lifts from farmers on quad bikes. And they're capable of reaching parts of the countryside over the sort of difficult terrain that quad bikes can only dream of.

Pastoral breeds include: Border collies, German shepherds and Welsh corgis.

Terrier

Bred for vermin control, terriers are tenacious. Don't start a tug-of-war game with one, for their stubbornness will win every time. Once their jaws have clamped onto something, they won't let go. Anything you dangle, you do so at your own risk when in front of a terrier. Men should therefore be careful when relieving themselves outdoors, anywhere near this watchful breed. Some of them are also expert diggers and will happily chase prey underground, through tunnels and dens, hoping to corner them so that they can go in for the kill. It also means that they are handy earthmovers, so gardeners who need a lot of double-digging and soil redistribution favour these animals.

Terrier breeds include: Jack Russell, West Highland, Norfolk, Australian and Yorkshire. Larger terrier breeds include Airedale, Irish and Staffordshire bull.

Toy

Toy dogs can make the perfect first dog because of their size. (Bigger rodents exist.) Originally developed as lapdogs, today's celebrity culture has changed them into handbag-dogs. Although they are quite active, their short stride means it takes ages for them to cover any distance if a change of handbag is involved.

Popular toy breeds include: Chihuahua, Pekingese, Pomeranian and the bichon frisé. Don't underestimate them. They all punch well above their weight.

Working

Working dogs are those that go out from nine to five during the week, have weekends off, and hopefully retire before they need a hip replacement. They are the dogs that were bred for specific working purposes, such as guarding, sled-pulling or search and rescue. These animals are extremely intelligent, although some might think that their unquestioning devotion to duty makes this questionable. A search-and-rescue dog might spend hours on a cold, wet, dark, windswept mountainside, and the dog's reward for finding the stupid hiker who got lost in the first place is to get a pat on the head. Then again, human search-and-rescue volunteers don't even get to receive this, so, technically, the dog is ahead of the game.

Working dog breeds include: Dobermanns, Great Danes, Rottweilers and Newfoundlands.

Utility (also known as non-sporting)
Utility dogs are not categorised as such because they're good at cleaning the household laundry, or doing the ironing, but are essentially the breeds of dog that fall outside any of the other categories.

Utility breeds include: bulldogs, Dalmatians and poodles.

GIVE A DOG A BAD NAME

A would-be bluffer should quickly be able to tell how smitten an owner is with their dog by the anthropomorphic qualities they attribute to it. Often, they'll talk about their dog many more times than they will talk about their life partner. Whereas a dog is for life (and not just for Christmas as we are often reminded), a partner is more likely to do until something better comes along…usually another dog.

DOG NAMES

Dog owners spend more time agonising over what to call their four-legged friend than they do their own offspring. It isn't always easy to decide who you should pity more: a child called Deefor (D for dog), or a Labrador called Colin.

There are two tests a dog owner should apply to a potential name to identify suitability:

The sound check The potential name should be said loudly and firmly to identify whether the sound clashes

THE BLUFFER'S GUIDE TO DOGS

with any potential commands you might give the dog. A name like Fred sounds similar to the command 'bed' which could cause confusion if you want your dog to come to you, and not slink disconsolately off for an early night. Similarly, calling a dog Neil isn't a good idea if you plan on using the command 'heel' to encourage him to walk at your side. But then, calling a dog Neil just isn't a good idea anyway.

The embarrassment sound check When a dog misbehaves, it will usually be on the other side of the park. The owner will have to shout the dog's name at a decibel level higher than that of a low-flying Airbus. Alongside the decibel levels, owners should consider the potential embarrassment quotient of shouting, 'Fluffy! Leave that lady's leg alone and come back here, now!'

Genuine dog owners are instantly recognised by their choice of dog name. It will be one or two syllables at most and dog-appropriate. In a recent survey by an American pet insurance company,, the top five most popular names for male dogs were: Max, Jake, Buddy, Jack and Cody. The five top names for female dogs were: Molly, Bella, Daisy, Maggie and Lucy. Obviously it's a matter of personal choice, but you might be better advised to avoid some of the others in the top 50 such as Armani, Dior, Gucci, Prada and Chanel. Why? Well, let's be honest, naming dogs after luxury fashion brands is just somehow…wrong.

Recent advances in personal finance security mean

that caution should also be exercised when deciding on a dog's name. It needs to be fairly innocent-sounding because your bank might require it as part of their login procedure for online account access. Somehow Razors, Knuckles or Slasher isn't really going to fill your customer service rep with unalloyed confidence in your banking credentials. (That's assuming that you have the privilege of talking to a human being rather than a machine, but even the latter will probably have trigger words to set alarms ringing.)

KENNEL CLUB NAMES

Pedigree dogs have two names. They have their 'call name' (the name the owner calls it when it is misbehaving in the park – usually preceded by a four-letter expletive) and then there is the Kennel Club name. The UK Kennel Club permits names of up to 24 characters, whereas in the USA, where everything is bigger, the American Kennel Club permits names of up to 36 characters. A kennel club name means the dog's family history can be traced. Think of it like a *Who Do You Think You Are?* for dogs. Things like this become important when you're the 29th generation Chelsea collie descendant of the original Lassie, and you're auditioning for the 12th remake of *Lassie Come Home.* You will of course know that the collie in the first Lassie film was called Pal. That leaves 33 characters unused, which seems a bit of a waste. Incidentally, after an exhausting retirement siring much-coveted litters, Pal died in 1958 in Hollywood aged 18 (126 in dog years).

LOOK-A-LIKES

There is a common misconception that dogs look like their owners. They don't. It's their owners who choose to look like their dogs. There is more than coincidence underlying this phenomenon. Recent research from Bath Spa University shows that people are more likely to select dogs with physical features similar to their own. This was the conclusion of a recent experiment where people were asked to match pictures of dogs to their owners. Participants correctly matched the picture of the dog to the owner twice as often as they were wrong. Bluffers need to know this sort of information.

BREED-A-LIKES

While look-a-likes might be considered as devoted individuals with more time on their hands (or paws) than is healthy, breed-a-likes are an entirely different…er… breed. These people not only look like their dogs, but they behave and act in the same way as their dogs too.

No respectable nightclub would be complete without a heavily built, crop-haired bouncer snarling at the door. At home, his faithful Rottweiler, probably called Tyson, is a mirror image of his master. Of course, anyone who really understands the breed knows you won't find a bigger pair of softies around. Even if they do have faces that only a mother could love.

DOGS AS CHILD SUBSTITUTES

It doesn't take a psychologist to point out that some

owners keep pets as surrogate children. Indeed, taking on the responsibility of looking after a dog is good practice for the moment an owner might stop practising human procreation and start actually accomplishing it. Perspicacious prospective parents will have already observed the similarities in the techniques advanced by 'experts' on how to regain control of unruly dogs and how to regain control of unruly children. For example, the 'naughty step' type of social isolation behaviour training used in bringing up children is frequently mimicked in training dogs. The only difference is that the dog should be effectively isolated immediately the bad behaviour occurs. It is important too that this technique should only ever be used for very short periods; dogs and children are unlikely to learn anything during long periods in solitary confinement (except brooding resentment).

Bad behaviour is usually the result of both kinds of unruly animal-seeking attention. And scolding or admonishing the child or dog is effectively providing that attention. Thus many experts recommend ignoring bad behaviour and instead effusively praising good behaviour. So next time you see your neighbour's dog chewing the leg of an antique Hepplewhite chair, just ignore it. Your neighbour will thank you for it in the end.

Of course, the best way to cut down on bad behaviour is to keep them so busy that they don't have time to get into mischief. That means swimming on Mondays, running on Tuesdays, ball sports on Wednesdays, guiding on Thursdays, and Zumba on Fridays. That leaves ballet and parties for the weekends. As for the children, well they'll just have to fit in with the dog's busy social life.

GRIEVING FOR A FAITHFUL FRIEND

To lose such a close member of the family can be understandably devastating and dog owners should be consoled in the same way as if a close human relative had died. People who are not, or never have been, dog owners don't actually get this. Some are ignorant enough to think that the loss of a dog is actually a laughing matter, and wonder why they are threatened with physical violence as a result. Even bluffers, especially bluffers, should know that the death of a dog should be handled with compassion and sensitivity. The bereaved dog owner will never forget any gesture of sympathy and understanding.

Improvements in diets and health treatments mean that dogs are now living for longer than ever before, with many canines now surviving into their mid-to-late teenage years (look at Pal of the missing 33 characters). This is far longer than some human relationships exist.

The loss of a dog serves as a poignant reminder of the reasons for keeping one in the first place:

- They won't leave you for another human being (taking most of your stuff with them).

- A dog doesn't care which political party you voted for.

- A dog is the best exercise apparatus ever invented, and unlike a personal trainer, it doesn't cost £60 per hour and won't shout at you.

- A dog will tell you when there's a burglar in the house.

Grieving for a dog can begin before it has died, because an owner can make the decision to have their canine companion 'put to sleep', rather than allow it to experience too much pain and suffering. But many observers would say that this is actually to the dog's benefit. If the subject arises you can demonstrate your erudition by quoting the Czech writer Milan Kundera: 'Dogs do not have many advantages over people, but one of them is extremely important: euthanasia is not forbidden by law in their case; animals have the right to a merciful death.'

But this can nonetheless be a troubling time because most owners are reluctant to take this course of action, even though they know it's the right thing to do. Coming to terms with making this decision can be just as hard as coping with the loss of the dog. Independent experts are not convinced that married partners would agonise for quite as long if they were responsible for choosing euthanasia for their other half.

A dog owner's true devotion can often be measured by what happens to their dog's body after death. While they might bury human relatives in the local churchyard, or cremate them and scatter their ashes at a cherished beauty spot, dog owners might bury Fido closer by, in the garden, or keep his ashes in a box on the mantelpiece in the living room. Aunt Flo's ashes will usually be relegated to the attic, if she's lucky. And Uncle Ron often finds himself in the cocktail cabinet (where, given a choice, he'd probably prefer to be).

The average dog has the same IQ level as a three-year-old child. This means that most dogs are capable of operating your mobile phone and logging onto your social media accounts when you're not looking.

CANINE CHARACTERISTICS

While the people who know nothing about the subject will assume that a dog is an animal with four legs and a tail, you will, of course, understand that this description accurately describes any number of other animals too. To really understand what makes a dog a dog, a little biological lesson is required.

SENSE OF SMELL

A dog's sense of smell is not to be sniffed at. While the human brain is approximately 10 times bigger than a dog's (depending on the size of the dog and the human), the amount of brain power devoted to smell in a human is dwarfed by that of a dog. The average canine brain assigns 40 times more cognitive activity to smell than the typical human brain. So next time a dog sniffs your hand, it'll collect more data about where you've been, when you've been there and who you've been with than your supermarket loyalty card. It's just as well that they can't talk.

This remarkable canine sensory skill all comes down to what's up our noses. Or rather theirs. While we both have smell receptors nestling inside our nostrils, the average human has some 5 million of them. Our canine companions can have anything between 125 million and 300 million. It's not clear who counted them all, or how they managed to get a dog to sit still for that long, but let's face it, if humans had that many receptors up their nose they'd probably go round sniffing each others' bottoms too. This knowledge has enabled scientists to conduct various tests and declare that it is possible for a dog to detect one scent particle in a million particles of distilled water (apparently).

One reason why dogs have this super-smelling skill is down to survival. When a puppy is first born, its eyes are closed, because they are not yet fully developed. It is also deaf. The only way it can establish its surroundings is through smell, and the strongest scent will be that of its mother. It is what enables the puppy to find out which part of the mother's anatomy is likely to produce sustenance. The eyes of a newborn puppy may not open for another two weeks after birth, so the sense of smell is its only way of understanding its immediate environment.

WET NOSES

Those who actually paid attention in school biology and chemistry lessons will already know that it is the moisture on dogs' noses that allows them to analyse an aroma so efficiently. For it is this moisture that traps the scent molecules and then enables the dog to dissolve them for analytical purposes, as they make their way into the nostrils towards the receptive membranes. Nerve impulses take this data from the membranes to the brain for the final interpretation, thus permitting a dog to determine what another dog ate for lunch three weeks ago by sniffing …you've got it…that part which reveals that sort of vital information.

INTELLIGENCE

Studies suggest that the average dog has the same IQ level as a three-year-old child. This means that most dogs are capable of operating the set-top box, retuning your 40-inch 3D TV, and logging onto your social media networks when you're not looking. On a good day, they're also capable of thrashing you completely on the tablet version of *Angry Birds*.

A dog's brain is said to weigh, on average, 0.5% of their entire body weight, whereas a human brain weighs about 2% of our total body weight. What dogs are good at doing is using their brain to learn new tricks. Despite the proverb stating otherwise, it is possible for an old dog to learn new tricks…it just takes a bit longer to learn them.

THE MOUTH

Dogs love using their mouths, but they're even happier when they have something in it…like…well, anything that's handy really. The chewing action releases endorphins, which help to keep them calm and relaxed as well as keeping them happily occupied. So when a dog chews the carpet, or the remote control, or your

THE BLUFFER'S GUIDE TO DOGS

favourite shoes, it is merely chillaxing. The best advice is to let them get on with it, unless the chew happens to be something of value. In those circumstances don't attempt to retrieve it from the dog's mouth without having something more interesting to replace it with.

TONGUE

A dog might win by a nose, but their tongue lets them down completely. Their taste buds are in full working order as soon as they are born (unlike their eyes), but they only have 1,700 of them (you might legitimately speculate about who counts these things). We humans have approximately six times more taste buds on our muscular hydrostat. Despite this taste bud deficiency, dogs are capable of distinguishing between sweet and sour, which is why they like Chinese food. Actually, it's why they like any food (except sprouts).

What a dog's tongue lacks in tasting ability it makes up for in other ways. The tongue is a major grooming tool enabling the dog to reach body parts many other animals cannot reach (but would do if they could). It can curl backwards to produce a ladle effect, which helps them to lap water into their mouths, and it's a major part of the canine cooling system. When a dog exercises, the amount of blood flowing into the tongue can increase up to sixfold. Heat makes the blood vessels expand, drawing more blood into the tongue, causing it to swell and 'loll'. Cooler air or water passing over the surface of the tongue enables the heat to exchange, allowing the blood to cool, thus reducing the dog's body temperature. But it's usually well before this point that a dog will decide to lick your face, covering you in slobber.

TEETH

Like humans, dogs have two sets of teeth, but they lose their puppy teeth at around four months old. They have 10 more teeth than us, (that's 42, in case you're not sure how many you should have). Twelve of them are incisors, ideal for nibbling and chewing. They also have four canine teeth, perfect for puncturing, 16 premolars for tearing the meat off a bone and 10 molars for crushing. Try not to remember all that the next time a dog is gently 'mouthing' your hand, and don't look too closely when it is effortlessly splintering a raw bone in the garden.

HEARING

Dogs have a complicated hearing system, which sometimes fails to notice an owner shouting 'STAY!' when both are in the same room, yet can detect the rustle of Stilton being unwrapped up to a mile away.

Dogs use their hearing to identify the source of a sound and also to differentiate between similar noises. This was necessary when they had to hunt for their food. As a human, your hearing range falls between 20 hertz and 20 kilohertz, whereas a dog can hear between 40 hertz and 60 kilohertz. A dog whistle emits a noise between 23 and 54 kilohertz, which is why we can't hear it, and explains why 98.275% of dog whistles are returned to the retailer as faulty.

The shape of a dog's ear is important. Ears that stick

up collect sounds like satellite dishes, and are capable of detecting a noise 80 metres away, unlike human ears which are deaf to anything further away than 20 metres. And because dog ears can move independently of one another, they're capable of identifying a noise's location in 0.06 seconds. Effectively, it means the dog probably knows that you've broken wind before you do.

SIGHT

The reason dogs have such good noses is because the eyesight of many breeds isn't always completely reliable. Some breeds have better eyesight than others, which is somewhat reassuring in the case of guide dogs. Despite this, there are some circumstances when dogs' sight is invariably better than ours, for which they can thank their hunting ancestors.

While neither dog, nor human, can see anything in complete darkness, dogs have far better vision in low light conditions, which might explain why a dog will frequently wake up its owner just before dawn, expecting to go for a walk. What dogs can't see particularly well is detail, which explains why they probably wouldn't pass a driving test. Current guidelines state that humans have to be able to read a car number plate at a distance of 20 metres. For a dog to read the same number plate they would need to be 14 metres closer. State this with confidence, although how (or why) anyone can work it out with any degree of accuracy is a mystery.

While a dog's direct vision might sometimes be suspect, its peripheral vision is generally outstanding. Dogs have viewed the world in widescreen format since their wolf days, although the actual field of vision varies from breed to breed. Those with short noses and wide faces have a field of vision extending to about 200 degrees, compared to a human's 190 degrees. However, dogs with longer noses, whose eyes are further around the side of their heads, have a field of vision reaching up to 270 degrees. It's this wide-angle peripheral vision that enables dogs to spot any slight movement of potential interest, such as a rabbit emerging from a hole or a dishwasher being loaded.

Canine eyes can determine colours, but not at the same vibrancy as humans. They can determine blues, yellows and greys of various shades, but not the important traffic light colours of reds or greens, which is probably another reason why they wouldn't pass a driving test.

To sound knowledgable about this subject to dog people, simply drop the words 'nictitating membrane' into the conversation. This is a dog's third eyelid, which sweeps horizontally across their eye, a bit like a windscreen wiper, pushing moisture evenly across the eyeball. If a vet mentions these words to you, adding an extra one, 'infection', steel yourself for a sizeable bill.

LANGUAGE

It's not what a dog says, but how it says it that you should profess to understand. There are three main ways a dog will communicate with the world around him:

- through noise;
- by using body language; and
- by 'marking territory'.

BARKING

The attentive bluffer will already have noted that dogs don't just bark. They also growl, howl, whine, whimper and yelp. This narrow vocabulary conveys a lot of information. Barking is the commonest form of spoken communication and can be interpreted in many different ways. A dog may bark with excitement, especially if it knows it is going out for a walk. It might bark with frustration if it's standing by the back door waiting to go outside. It will bark in a very different tone if an intruder is trying to break in through the back door. Incessant barking, particularly by dogs who are left alone, is often a sign of boredom.

Growling can mean enjoyment, especially if it involves playing tug-of-war with something…like the cat next door or a human limb.

Howling harks back to the days of communicating with other dogs over vast distances. A dog will whimper, or yelp, when in pain or discomfort. A whining dog is like a teenager. It wants something – usually food or a new pair of trainers.

Growling is generally an expression of displeasure, although it can mean enjoyment, especially if it involves playing tug-of-war with something…like the cat next door or a human limb.

BODY LANGUAGE

A dog's body language is best understood by another dog, or somebody who really understands dog behaviour. While an ill-informed person might assume that a wagging tail is always a sign of friendliness, you as a bluffer will point out that this is not necessarily the case. Depending upon the height of the tail, and how much of it is wagged, the message can be interpreted differently. A tail that is hung low and wags frantically suggests the dog is experiencing a sense of anxiousness and uncertainty. However, recent studies by the Italian universities of Trieste and Bari have suggested that a dog's tail wags with a bias towards the right when it is happy and with a bias to the left if it is uncertain, or nervous. Note that these studies refer to the dog's left and right, not yours as you face the dog. So, it's all right if the dog's tail wags to your left, but it might be a problem if it wags to your right. Make sure that you're clear on this.

A threatening dog will communicate its message in many ways. It will snarl, draw back its lips to show its teeth, and point its tail high into the air. It will also stare at you, raise its hackles, and stand tall, in an attempt to dominate the situation. An unthreatening dog will indulge in all sorts of different body language, ranging from lying submissively on its back to jumping up and trying to lick your ears. Rest assured that you'll quickly learn the difference between threatening and non-threatening behaviour. If in doubt turn your back and stand still. Or put a closed door between you and the dog.

SCENT MARKING

Dogs use both urine and faeces to leave scent markers to other dogs. Not only does this scent help them to mark out their territory, but scent also informs other dogs of the sex, health and status of the urinating/defecating dog. A male dog will cock a leg to urinate on a vertical surface to mark his scent at the height of other dogs' noses. Female dogs are more likely to squat, usually in the middle of a carefully manicured lawn where they take pleasure in leaving a perfectly concentric pattern of burns as intricate as a crop circle.

DINNER TIME

Grey wolves did not kill a couple of bison, take them home, and cook them on the top shelf of the oven at gas mark nine for 20 minutes, before turning it down to gas mark three for 20 minutes for every 200 grams in weight. Nor did they boil Brussels sprouts for eight minutes to get just the right consistency of crunchiness. In fact, the preferred canine diet is raw and largely carniverous.

THE BARF DIET

There is controversy over the best way to feed a domestic dog. The subject tends to inflame dog owners' passions, (not to mention their dogs'), and you should know enough to make an intelligent, informed comment about it. Should you hear a dog owner refer to the BARF diet, do not assume it is some kind of canine bulimic vomiting diet.

BARF stands for Biologically Appropriate Raw Food. Exponents believe that giving their dogs a diet that mirrors what they naturally ate in the wild is the kindest and healthiest way to feed their dog. Some believe it gives their dogs a longer life, fewer degenerative diseases like cancers, heart conditions and Alzheimer's, as well as a shinier glossier coat. ('Because they're worth it', of course). The ingredients of a BARF diet include:

- bones with meat on them (T-bone steak, pork ribs);

- offal (internal organs and entrails); and

- crushed vegetables (usually found in the digestive system of a recently deceased herbivore).

However, opponents claim that this makes it difficult for the dog to obtain a balanced diet full of the right nutrients and vitamins at the right time. Giving dogs uncooked bones also increases the risk of the bone splintering and causing damage as it passes through the dog's digestive system. BARF supporters (if they have the misfortune to be known as such) claim that uncooked bones don't splinter. BARF objectors counter that owners who feed this raw diet to their dogs often supplement it with cheeses and yoghurt, fruits and herbs, which might be good news for delicatessens but isn't likely to bring much joy to the dogs. If you're a fan of *Wallace & Gromit* you can probably guess which part of the deli-diet the dog eats first.

DRIED AND WET FOOD

The more common diet for dogs (apart from leftovers and whatever indulgent owners surreptitiously slip under the table at meal times) is dog food prepared by pet food manufacturers, which is classified as either 'wet' or 'dried'. Wet dog food is sloppy and messy and usually comes out of a tin or pouch. Dried dog food comes in the guise of very boring biscuits, sometimes bone-shaped to make them more interesting. However boring the latter might be, they nonetheless comprise a nutritionally balanced diet designed to give dogs supple joints, a healthy heart and, of course, a glossy coat. There is a school of thought that suggests that a human being could survive on such a diet and lead a relatively long life. But they probably wouldn't look forward to mealtimes much. Neither do dogs, so it's often a good idea to perk up the offering with a sprinkling of cheese or some leftovers.

Wet dog food can look and smell as though it uses a higher quality of meat than might be found in some human ready-meal dishes. Given a choice between chicken nuggets or turkey twizzlers and a tin of dog food, most of us would probably opt for the dog food, which is also frequently more palatable than the standard offering in a school canteen. Owners who prefer wet dog food also like the fact that portion size is standard, which means that the dog is fed the same quantity each day.

Dry dog food has been pre-cooked (beyond recognition), which evaporates much of the moisture content and is then left to dry further. Vitamins and minerals are sometimes sprayed over these biscuit-like pieces to increase their nutritional value. It's easy to overfeed a dog on dried dog food because nutritionally, a smaller quantity of food is required. And recommended servings are likely to be far in excess of what the dogs need; but, guess what? More dog food will be sold.

The sure-fire way to tell the difference between a dog fed on wet food and one fed on dried food is to smell its breath. Wet dog food breath can knock a policeman off his bike at 200 metres, and you really don't want to get downwind of it. You certainly don't need to employ all five million of your smell receptors to tell what they've been eating.

FATAL FOODS

The improvements in the nutritional value of dog food have helped to increase the life expectancy of dogs. However, there are some foods (including some raw foods) that dogs should avoid. Chocolate contains theobromine, which is also found in the leaves of tea plants, and cannot be processed by dogs efficiently. It dilates the blood vessels, which is why humans enjoy eating it because it lowers blood pressure. It's also diuretic. It is possible for humans to die from theobromine poisoning, although this generally happens to older people if they consume excessively large quantities of chocolate. (So unless you want to see them off, it's not a good idea to give elderly relatives a tin of Quality Street at Christmas.) The levels of theobromine halve in the human body within 10 hours, whereas in a dog it can take up to 17 hours.

Raw onions, including garlic, should be avoided because the chemical thiosulphate contained within them causes the red blood cells to explode, leading to anaemia.

Macadamia nuts have been found to cause muscle problems, leading to difficulties with standing and moving about, while grapes and raisins can lead to renal failure. Therefore, in the interest of a dog's health, they should be kept off the grape.

The same could be said about many of their owners.

Allowing a dog to drink stagnant pond water is not good for the dog's digestive system, nor for the owner's living room shagpile carpet.

WATER

Dogs need a good supply of water every day. Responsible owners will carry fresh water with them at all times. You can always tell how much an owner values their dog by the brand of mineral water they carry for them. To the non-dog owner, bottled water may appear a little extravagant for a dog. However, allowing a dog to drink stagnant pond water is not good for the dog's digestive system, nor for the owner's living room shagpile carpet when the microscopic bugs breeding in water are expelled from the other end…often before the dog, or owner, realises what's going on. And it's not a good idea to let dogs drink from roadside puddles. They're often contaminated with petrol, diesel, or antifreeze – none of which is likely to be much good for the dog.

Most tap water is as good if not better than designer mineral waters. And, to be honest, dogs don't actually like the sparkling variety.

To test whether a dog is dehydrated, use a finger and thumb to pull at the skin at the back of a dog's neck. When you let go, the skin should return to its flated state, quickly. If it takes more than three seconds, the dog is dehydrated. This is a useful trick to know, but it only really works with short-haired dogs. And if you haven't got one, and attempt to demonstrate the technique to the owner of a short-haired dog, they are unlikely to be over-impressed at the inference that their dog is not properly hydrated. And the dog probably won't be too happy at having its neck tugged. But you never know... there might be an occasion when you can demonstrate your knowledge and experience of these things to an attractive member of the opposite sex with a heavily panting dog in the park, before administering some refreshing mineral water. (We all have our dreams....)

FEEDING

Teething puppies appear to be feeding all the time – on chair legs, table legs and human legs, but this is merely to relieve the discomfort caused when puppy teeth are lost and adult teeth push through. Puppies need to be fed frequently, up to four times a day until they're three months old, and then three times a day until they're six months old. After that, twice a day is recommended, feeding a third of their daily intake for breakfast, with the remaining two-thirds in the evening. Whereas humans should apparently breakfast like a king, lunch like a lord and dine like a pauper, dogs do the reverse. The only thing they have in common with kings and lords is that humans serve their food. And dogs, like aristocracy, rarely bother to offer to help with the washing-up – unless it's a pre-wash of the contents of the dishwasher.

Feeding time is a good indicator as to who is the alpha male or female in the pack, generally the animal or human who eats before everybody else. Owners might say that feeding the dog first allows them to eat their meal without a slobbering muzzle on their thigh, but that's only because they have been trained by the dog to satisfy its needs first before those of the rest of the family. It knows that if it is fed first, there's always the opportunity for 'bonus' material from what's left on the family plates.

OBESITY

Fat dogs are not just increasing in size, but in numbers too. The Association for Pet Obesity Prevention in the USA identified that of the 41 million dogs in the country, about 45% are overweight or obese. When owners were asked if they thought their dog was obese, only 17% said yes.

Some vets blame this increasing problem on a feeding strategy called 'free-choice', where food is made available to the dog at all times of the day and it is trusted to stop eating when its instincts tell it that to eat more would be unhealthy. Fat chance. This is arguably one of the most ill-conceived theories in the history of the science of dog behaviour. It is based on the principle that the dog's wolf ancestors could go out and eat as much as they wanted at any time of day and yet didn't have a problem with obesity. This might have had something to do with wolves not having a handy human on hand with a tin of food and a can opener, and the fact that they didn't know when or where the next meal was coming from. They would also have to expend considerable time and physical effort to find their food, unlike a domesticated dog which gets fed whether it exercises or not.

The solution is simple: eat less and exercise more. And that goes for the dogs too.

PUPPY POWER

By the age of three, your dog is a mature adult. At seven years old he is in middle age and by the age of 10 he is heading towards his twilight years. Puppies can be like children: lovely to play with for 10 minutes, but unrelenting in their demands on your time and attention. It is sometimes tempting to hand them back to their owner, until you remember that's you.

What many dog owners also forget is that all puppies turn into teenagers at some point. The better trained they are during the puppy years, the less terrible the teenaged years are likely to be.

PUPPY-PROOFING

Before any new owner brings home their bundle of fun and mischief, they have to puppy-proof their home. This means blocking up holes in garden fences, putting wire baskets around the letter box to protect postmen's fingers, concealing extension leads and loose electrical wires, and getting rid of houseplants that are poisonous

(African violets, rubber plants, poinsettias and, perhaps unsurprisingly, mother-in-law's tongue). For many, this is an inconvenience, however the more astute owner will see it as a brilliant opportunity to dispose of a few unwanted wedding gifts. There are so many vases, lamps, statues and other objets d'art at convenient tail-wagging height that just happen to get knocked over and smashed beyond repair. Owners can blame as much as they like on the dog, and yet the dog will continue to love them unconditionally. One of the great advantages of noble hounds is that they don't understand the concept of buck-passing.

TRAINING

You would do well to remember that there is no such thing as a badly behaved dog, only bad owners. Owners must be in control of their dogs at all times. When a dog is chasing and worrying sheep, the farmer has the legal right to shoot the dog. Yet, ironically, it is not the dog that is at fault here. Very few natural herding dogs can control their instincts without proper training, and it is the human owner who is responsible for not being in control of his hound. You wouldn't be the first to think that perhaps the farmer should have the right to shoot the owner instead.

A good bluffer will state solemnly that it is a dog owner's responsibility to ensure that they train their dog to the best of their ability. Those who take this responsibility seriously will seek out extra help in the form of The Kennel Club's Good Citizen Dog Scheme. (The American Kennel Club has a similar Canine Good Citizen test.) This is where the dog owners are trained in how to train their dogs. The trainers themselves have training on how to train owners to train their dogs, but it isn't entirely clear who trains the trainers who train the trainers who train the owners to train their dogs. (It's probably a pack of timber wolves in Nova Scotia.)

HOUSE TRAINING

House training is all about teaching dogs to go outside the house when they need to do their 'business'. As someone who purports to know about dogs, you will also know not to shilly-shally about the precise terminology to use in describing this particular act. Going outside for a 'wee' or a 'poo' is perfectly acceptable. Lazy humans, reluctant to clean up every morning after their puppy, might be tempted to invest in puppy 'training pads' or nappies. Don't. It's not going to be a workable long-term solution, and is likely only to delay the training process.

You will learn to accept that puppies need to empty their bladder:

- as soon as they wake up;
- at least every two hours during the day;
- after eating and drinking;
- after playing and excitement; and
- before going to bed.

In other words, all the time.

A good owner should always heap praise on a puppy when it has a bowel or bladder movement in the appropriate place. You might think a celebratory dance and song in the garden is a little over the top, but if you've spent the last six weeks cleaning out the seagrass in the sitting room with cotton buds, even the most minor of tiddles outside is a major breakthrough.

Nobody's dog is perfect
(except yours, obviously – even if
he/she has put on a little weight).

LURE AND REWARD

Let's face it, the best way to get anyone to do something they don't want to do is to bribe them. The 'lure and reward' training system rewards the dog for doing what their owner wants them to do. Typical rewards include verbal praise, petting and stroking, playing games and food. Rewards should be varied, but cat chasing is not one that is officially recognised by trainers and behaviour experts. While rewarding with treats is perfectly acceptable, these should be used sparingly. If you find yourself running out on a regular basis, and your dog is no longer able to wriggle under the stile, then you've almost certainly overdone it. You'll know for sure when fellow dog owners start speaking in 'fattist' euphemisms (as in: 'He's looking well fed these days,' 'Is she pregnant,' and 'So still got the winter coat on then?'). Ignore them. Nobody's dog is perfect (except yours, obviously – even if he/she has put on a little weight).

When training goes well, humans introduce hand signals as a way of issuing commands. If you see any of the following, it means that a human is communicating with their dog (or others):

- An upturned hand, held out in front, is brought up towards the shoulder: **sit**.

- An outstretched arm, with a pointed finger, moves downwards to point at the floor: **down**.

- A palmed hand held out to face the dog: **stay**.

- Two fingers stuck up (probably at someone for speculating about your dog's weight): **sod off**.

- One finger stuck up (at someone who criticises your dog in any other way): **swivel on it**.

CLICKER TRAINING

Strictly speaking, every time someone uses a clicker to reward a dog, a fish should be involved. Clicker training began in marine parks to teach dolphins to perform tricks and backflips for an audience. The click was used to indicate that a rewarding fishy treat would be heading their way soon. Someone realised that this would work for dogs, too.

The sound of the click tells the dog that they've done something right immediately, and that a reward will follow. One click is enough. Any more than that and the dog might think you're a dolphin.

DOG WHISPERING

A dog whisperer is often a smarmy snake-oil-salesman type who is capable of getting your dog to do something you couldn't imagine getting him to do – often without uttering a word. These people are the ultimate dog bluffers and must therefore be respected, admired and even emulated. You need know nothing at all about dogs, but if you can persuade one to do something for you that it won't do for its owner, then you will earn the undying respect and admiration of both. How it is done is a mystery, but it probably has something to do with a previously negotiated deal between dog and whisperer to perform apparent miracles. Large quantities of black-market liver pâté and strong cheese have been known to change hands to lend credence to the illusion.

Whisperers generally work on the principle that 93% of all communication is through body language, with oral communication taking up the remaining 7%. During an hour's training session a dog whisperer will only whisper four words, usually at the end: 'That'll be £300, please.'

ESSENTIAL ACCESSORIES

Any dog will tell you that the best accessory is a human being, but there are a number of others. A passing familiarity with these will persuade your audience that you understand the very basics of dog ownership. You might need, for example:

Barriers Stair gates are useful for stopping dogs and puppies from exploring beds and bedrooms, but only if you have stairs. If there is one area in the home that should be barred to dogs it is upstairs. If it isn't, they will make your bed their bed.

Bowls A minimum of two are required: one for fresh water and one for food. They can be stainless steel, ceramic or plastic. They all make an excruciating noise as they're pushed around the kitchen floor by a hungry dog, so make sure they're fairly heavy, and it's not a bad idea to place them on a rubber mat. Alternatively you can invest in something called a 'dual dining set' with an adjustable height mechanism for each stainless steel bowl, depending on the size of the dog. These tend to take up quite a lot of room, but they do look rather fetching in a hi-tech kitchen.

Crate A strong metal cage, which can be used as a den, or to transport your dog safely in the back of the car when travelling. Remember that it's the dog's private space and not a jail, so don't use it for isolating the dog when he has misbehaved. Otherwise he will, quite understandably, refuse to use it for sleeping.

Dog collar If you happen to know a friendly vicar, ask if he/she has got a spare one. Actually, don't. Vicars hear more dog-collar 'jokes' than any other. All you need to know about a collar is that it should go around a dog's neck, and that it should be comfortable and loose, but not so loose that you can pull it over the dog's head.

'Choke' collars, which tighten as the dog pulls, are ill-advised because they can damage the windpipe and delicate throat muscles, and 'shock' collars should only be used by professional trainers as a last resort. You should express strong views about these things, and if some idiot claims to know that a shock collar is actually painless – call his bluff and offer to try it on him and see how much he enjoys a dose of 'tough love'.

First-aid kit Not always for the dog, but frequently for the owner. Being pulled through stinging nettles, under low-hanging branches, through bushes, into lampposts, and tripped down some steps can cause wear and tear on the human body. For the dog, it's not a bad idea if you're on a long walk to take a sterile wipe, some gauze, and some binding tape. Dogs can injure their paw pads on sharp stones or glass, and when they do, you can guarantee it will be at the furthest point from home. Note that if the bandage needs to be kept in place for any length of time, don't invest in an expensive weatherproof dog 'boot' which your vet will be keen to sell you. A golf club cover will do just as well, for a fraction of the cost. Bluffers need to know these things.

Grooming/bathing kit Like it or not, a dog's fur needs brushing and combing from time to time, especially if it's of the heavy-coated variety. So have a comb, brush and some dog shampoo handy. Although fur is naturally self-cleaning, that doesn't mean it never needs washing. This is especially true if the dog has rolled in fox droppings.

You'll know when this happens, and so will everyone within a radius of about 500 metres. Apart from the horrible distinctly acrid odour, fox excrement commonly contains mites and other burrowing parasites. When the subject arises, you might take advantage of the moment to explain why no dog can resist rolling in the stuff. It's fairly simple: they do it instinctively to mask their scent when hunting. The only flaw in this argument is that whatever they're hunting can smell them from the next county.

Harness This is an apparatus which fits around the chest and is safer for dogs that consistently pull. It is also less likely to break than a collar. They are not the first choice for a dog, but they're infinitely preferable to anything that tightens around the throat.

Lead These come in two sizes: short, for when walking a dog to heel close by your side; and long, for those times when you want to trip up crowds of people on the pavement. A retractable model makes the most sense, and then you can do both.

Old towels You can never have too many old towels. And very soon you will find that you will indeed have many old towels. Once used on a dog, there is a natural human reluctance ever to use the towel again on yourself.

Poop bags Bluffers will claim never to buy special dog poop bags. Nappy bags are about a third of the price, are nicely perfumed, and do the job just as well.

Toys All dogs have a favourite toy. It's the one you happen to be holding at any moment in time. Dogs frequently have more toys than children, and like children they spend much of their time scattering them around the place in many different pieces. Bluffers should bear in mind that they have two different functions: they are distractions and they are rewards. If they are just left lying discarded about the place, then your dog is less likely to value them. Much the same as with the kids.

HEALTH AND SAFETY

Dogs would be so much more relaxed if vets didn't call their places of work 'practices'. If vets need guinea pigs to practise on, then dogs would much rather that particular job was left to the guinea pigs. Veterinary practices have health implications for humans, too. Most vets' bills are capable of causing stroke or coronary thrombosis.

TABLETS

Dogs that are prescribed tablets enjoy playing the avoidance game. Humans don't, and it usually takes three steps to get a dog to ingest a pill:

Step 1 Using two hands, one human will hold open the dog's top and bottom jaws as wide as possible. A second human will throw the tablet into the back of the dog's mouth. The dog will use their tongue to flick the tablet back across the kitchen floor. The excess saliva produced during this process means the tablet has probably begun to disintegrate, and a second attempt is therefore impossible.

THE BLUFFER'S GUIDE TO DOGS

Step 2 The human hides the tablet in amongst the food in the dog's dinner bowl. With their exceptional sense of smell, dogs detect this subterfuge and simply eat around the tablet.

Step 3 Finally, after two days of trying, the owner will take a piece of cheese, wrap it around the tablet and give it to the dog, which it will happily swallow. For some strange reason, owners always go through steps 1 and 2, when it would be simplest to go straight to step 3.

PLASTIC COLLARS

Dogs that are recovering from surgery are often given protective collars in the shape of cones to wear to prevent them irritating stitches or wounds. This isn't always comfortable for the dog, because it interferes with their ability to hear and smell. It also prevents them attending to that part of their anatomy which they devote more time to than anywhere else. These days it is possible to buy inflatable collars which are supposed to do a similar job, even if they do have the effect of making the dog look like an extra from an Elizabethan restoration drama.

INJECTIONS, VACCINATIONS AND BOOSTERS

Even the healthiest dog can't escape a visit to the vet. During the first few weeks of life, puppies are inoculated against various diseases such as canine distemper, hepatitis, parvovirus, leptospirosis and sometimes kennel cough. These vaccinations need to be topped up regularly, some on an annual basis, others every three years. These top-up vaccinations are known as 'boosters', probably because they boost the vet's profits. While the injections may be momentarily painful for the dog, they are considerably more painful for their owners, who could have spent the money on a luxury holiday instead.

NEUTERING

The well-known phrase 'the dog's bollocks' means 'simply the best'. It came about because something that takes that much licking has got to be good, and if there's one thing that receives a lot of licking it's, well, you know what…

It's a fact of life that male dogs are not known for taking a responsible approach to parenthood.

So castration is a subject that should always be whispered in the presence of a dog, or not in its presence at all. Rescue centres commonly neuter dogs, and it's a sensible precaution to take to prevent unwanted pregnancies. Although it might seem a little harsh, it's a fact of life that male dogs are not known for taking a responsible approach to parenthood and are difficult to pin down when it comes to maintenance payments.

Neutering is an emotional subject, especially for the dog. Although there is plenty of evidence to suggest that spaying a female before she first comes into season can raise life expectancy by up to 18 months (by eliminating the possibility of some life-threatening illnesses), there is no such compensation for a male dog. Being told that it will be less inclined to mount anything from a large stuffed toy to a tortoise is unlikely to be much of a consolation.

UNDERSTANDING VETERINARY JARGON

Most veterinarians are keen to remind you that they have spent anywhere between five and eight years training to learn a different language and then charge you lots of money. Here's some help decoding:

Ataxia Means wobbly. Your dog may have difficulty standing or walking properly. Translation: very expensive.

BAER Brain auditory-evoked response. Translation: a hearing test.

Castration Neutering your male dog. Translation: authorise it and he'll look at you mournfully for the rest of his life.

Dysplasia Abnormal tissue development. Translation: extremely expensive.

Hypertrophic osteodystrophy Translation: painful and swollen joints and bones.

Lens luxation Eyesight disorder that can lead to glaucoma. Translation: not suitable as a guide dog for the blind.

Mitral valve defect A heart defect. Translation: very, very expensive.

Oestrus The stage at which a female dog is most receptive to mating. Translation: Break out your wallet. Lots of puppies to vaccinate.

Sebaceous adenitis Inflammation of the hair follicles and oil glands. Translation: the dog might need to attend a health spa on a weekly basis.

PET INSURANCE

Pet insurance is just like any other insurance; it only seems to pay out when there isn't a vowel in the month. Most dog owners take out pet insurance simply because one step into a vets clinic can cost the price of a small family car.

Vets argue that advances in medicine and surgical techniques mean they're capable of doing far more to improve and prolong a dog's quality of life. Recent studies have shown that a dog that is unable to walk because of spinal injuries can have cells taken from the lining of its nose and injected into its damaged spine, repairing some of the damage. Paralysed dogs are learning how to walk again – further proof that dogs' noses really are remarkable.

With no such thing as a National Health Service for animals, it can be a little galling when a dog only has to wait three days for a hip operation, whereas its owner has to endure a six-month waiting list if he/she doesn't have private medical insurance. However, it can be enormously satisfying completing a claim form when the cost of surgery runs into £1,000s. Suddenly those monthly premiums of £50-plus can seem like remarkably good value.

Like other insurance, policy cover varies. Some policies only pay out up to a set limit, and when that is reached the policy comes to an end and the company is unlikely to reinsure the dog. For cash-strapped owners, the end of the policy can spell the end of the dog too, although rescue centres will try to help out if they can. Other policies pay out up to a set limit each year, which is better suited to those dogs who only fall ill in November and December. Those who fall ill in January and February and use up their limit may not be quite so lucky. The gilt-edged policies which pay out with no limit for ongoing health problems are usually accompanied by gilt-edged premiums.

Insurers don't like old dogs. Older dogs are more expensive and make costlier claims, so they often refuse to insure a dog over 10 years old. You might raise an eyebrow at the irony of a system that will pay out huge sums of money to help dogs reach a ripe old age, but will refuse to insure them when they reach it.

DOGNAPPING

There can be serious money at stake when dogs are stolen and then held to ransom. Distraught dog owners have been known to remortgage their houses to pay ransoms of up to £50,000 for the safe return of a much-loved hound. The most money made out of a successful instance of dognapping was by Walt Disney Productions: its film, *101 Dalmatians*, became the 10th-highest grossing film of 1961, and that's not counting the millions earned from stuffed toys. With some pedigree dogs costing several thousands of pounds, dog thefts are on the increase, which raises the question: do dogs

---

Smaller designer dogs are popular targets simply because they're easier to bundle into a getaway car than a Great Dane.

---

need guard dogs? During times of economic downturn, the number of dog thefts increases dramatically. Smaller designer dogs are popular targets simply because they're easier to bundle into a getaway car than a Great Dane. There's also an outside chance that it might belong to a vacuous celebrity with more money than sense who's noticed that their handbag is suddenly lighter.

Part of the problem with dognapping, and the reason that it is a growth industry, is that the police don't take it very seriously – unless it's a police dog of course, in which case a full-scale doghunt will be launched with up to 200 officers and a couple of helicopters. Another problem is that it's difficult to distinguish between a dognapper and a genuinely good citizen when someone turns up on your doorstep with the missing dog, a story about where they found it, and hand it back claiming the reward money. Actually, it's not that difficult, because the good citizen is unlikely to be standing there with his hand out. On the other hand, most owners don't care, and are so pathetically grateful that they'll hand over the advertised reward without a murmur.

MICROCHIPPING

Up to one in every three dogs goes missing at some point during their lifetime, with only 17% finding their way back home. One of the quickest ways to reunite a missing dog with its rightful owner is to ensure that the dog is microchipped. This sensible precaution can also be used to prevent thefts. The chip, no larger than a grain of rice, is inserted into the dog under the skin between the shoulder blades, and carries a unique number. This number is registered to the dog, with its owner's details logged onto a central database accessible by vets, animal rescue charities, and the police. The chip also has one other major advantage from a dog's point of view. They have integral thermometers, which mean that a dog's body temperature can be read by a handheld scanning device rather than by ramming a thermometer up the back passage.

FUN AND GAMES

EXERCISE

A dog should not become a couch 'pet-ato'. It needs regular exercise and mental stimulation. Different breeds require different amounts of exercise. Toy dogs, such as Pekingese and chihuahuas, require very little exercise. Jumping in and out of a handbag all day might be all the exercise they need. Lurchers or Border collies, on the other hand/paw, think nothing of doing a couple of marathons before breakfast.

The best form of exercise is one that dog and owner can do together, which is why dog walking is so popular. But in a modern society, a walk in the park is exactly that: a walk in the park. Twenty-first-century dogs require twenty-first-century exercise. Welcome to the world of canicross, or CaniX, to those in the know.

CaniX

CaniX means running with your dog, not chasing it halfway across town in the desperate hope of catching it up. To take part in competitions, human runners have to be at least seven years old, while dogs have to be one year old (or seven in dog years). Courses can be of various lengths and gradients to suit the dog's capabilities (and those of the human, too).

No special equipment is required, although many participants buy a running harness. This goes around the dog's chest and shoulder blades and is attached to the human's waist by a bungee stretch cord. When the human tires, they simply allow the dog to do all of the pulling. That's fine in principle, until the dog shoots off course, pulling its human co-runner face first through several fields in pursuit of a fox. A large part of CaniX is coming to terms with the dog's ability to cross the finish line relatively clean, while their co-runners look like they've just participated in the world bog-snorkelling championships.

Mushing

Owners who can't be bothered to run with their dogs might opt for mushing, or dog sledding, instead. Being pulled as a passenger can in theory be done with one dog, although expecting a corgi to pull anything bigger than a shoebox is asking for trouble. The more dogs you have, the faster you can travel – over a surprising distance. The greatest mushing trail is arguably the Iditarod, a trek of nearly 1,000 miles across Alaska.

Stick/Ball Throwing

After walking, the commonest form of exercising a dog is by throwing a stick or a ball. No surprise there then. Bluffers should state that sticks are never a good idea.

In fact, more injuries are caused to dogs by impaling themselves on sticks or collecting splinters in their mouths than any other recreational activity. Balls are less dangerous, but you should ensure that it is big enough that it cannot be swallowed.

The Great Outdoors

The great outdoors is full of exciting opportunities for dogs and dog walkers. You might have noticed how often it is a dog walker who comes across a dead body hidden in the undergrowth. In truth it is rarely the dog walker who makes the discovery, and nearly always the dog – but it is an example of yet another vital service provided by our faithful mutts. If it weren't for dogs the countryside would be littered with hundreds of undiscovered corpses.

Barriers to Dog Walking

A walk in the park isn't always a stroll in the park. Exercising a dog can be challenging. Take stiles, for example. These are designed to prevent sheep and cattle from wandering between fields, while allowing walkers to cross over a hedge, or stone wall. Stiles can be difficult for two-legged people to negotiate, let alone anything with four legs. The easiest solution is to pick up the dog and carry it over. Stiles can always be found next to the muddiest of puddles. This is so the dog is caked in mud and slurry for that precise moment when you have to lift it over.

Advanced stiles include 'dog gates'. These are slats of wood that can be raised to create an aperture for the dog to nip through. Most assume your dog has not eaten anything for the past three weeks, or is the size of a chihuahua, which is ridiculous, because it if was a chihuahua it would be in your rucksack, not on the ground.

'Kissing gates' confuse dogs. They also confuse many people.

Particularly boggy areas are sometimes equipped with boardwalks. These are ribbed structures that float on top of marshy sections, and are not dissimilar to cattle grids. Dogs hate them both, and you will find that invariably you will be required to carry the dog again.

Avoid dog coats at all times.
Real dogs don't wear them.

WALKING WEATHER

There is no such thing as bad weather, only bad clothing (as the saying goes). It's at this point that dog owners suddenly marvel at their faithful companions. For no matter what the weather is doing outside, a dog is always appropriately dressed and ready to go. A typical human needs to consider the following:

- How cold is it outside? Is thermal underwear required?

- Is it raining? How heavy is the rain? Will a showerproof jacket suffice, or does the jacket need to be hurricane-proof?

- Trousers. These should be dark-coloured so they don't show the dog's muddy paw prints – and waterproof, naturally.

- Gloves, hat and scarf. Where did I put them the last time I wore them?

- Feet. How many pairs of socks are required?

- Feet again. Which shoes? Wellington boots, trainers, walking shoes, or walking boots?

Dogs just wear the same clothes inside and out, all the time. Much simpler. And bluffers should know to avoid dog coats at all times. Real dogs don't wear them.

PULLING POWER

There is an aspect of dog walking relating to sex (of the human variety) that many dog owners enjoy. No, not 'dogging' as in the voyeuristic practice of observing the act of copulation between humans in a public place. (Although walking in certain areas of the countryside can provide such opportunities…apparently.)

Dogs have pulling power. This is not a technical term for the torque applied to a lead, but refers to the dog's ability to attract a human of the opposite (or even the same) sex to its owner. Women who see a man walking a dog, see someone who is prepared to take on a commitment and work at a relationship. Men who see a woman walking a dog see someone who understands and appreciates the pleasure of tactile interaction. Many a successful human relationship has begun with two pairs of eyes meeting over a hairy mutt.

SHEEP WORRYING

This is not about telling sheep that their pensions will be worthless. Instead it is about sheep worrying that they might be attacked by dogs. And worry they should, because police records show that attacks are on the increase.

Any dog can find its natural wolf-like instincts kicking in at the sight of a sheep. There's a grey wolf inside every dog, even one that spends most of its time in a handbag. You might think that your family pet wouldn't hurt a fly, but if it was desperate enough it would kill for food without hesitation. If it was hungry enough, it might even eat you.

It's the chase that arouses the primeval wolf-instinct in a dog, and it's the chase that causes a sheep to worry that its days could be numbered. Dogs don't have to physically attack a sheep to be guilty of worrying it, they simply need to be running around the field barking. A sheep can die purely from anxiety, and dead sheep are lost income for farmers. This is why the law permits them to shoot dogs without a warning, without reading them their rights, and without a trial. It's called summary justice. Owners should be worried about sheep worrying, too. Not only might they lose their dog, but they might find themselves on the wrong end of a hefty fine – or even a prison sentence.

THE ALLURE OF OTHER ANIMALS' FAECES

The great outdoors is a repository of a myriad different irresistible smells for dogs – particularly those which emanate from other creatures' droppings. With 300 million smell receptors twitching in anticipation, dogs are spoilt for choice in this respect, and can happily occupy themselves for hours distinguishing between an alpaca turd and a squirrel stool. Few sensory experiences give them greater pleasure.

DOG TOYS

Dog toys are designed to entertain and stimulate a dog, but there are several that can be bought to encourage and stimulate play between a dog and their owner:

- *Balls* As advised earlier, balls should be large enough not to be swallowed, and not too hard to hurt a dog if it is accidentally hit by one. Ball-launchers are ideal for owners who (a) can't throw, (b) don't want to pick up soggy balls, or (c) both. It's a long plastic curved arm that cups the ball at one end, requiring less human effort to throw the ball long distances. The downside is, if the dog can't be bothered to fetch the ball, the owner has further to walk to to get it back.

- *Rubber sticks* These are long rubber 'twizzle'-shaped 'sticks' which don't splinter in a dog's mouth, don't spear it in the abdomen, and also have the advantage of floating in water (which means that they can double as a life-saving aid if the dog can be persuaded to let them go). Bluffers should say that they are an eminently sensible recent introduction to the ever-growing arsenal of toys in the dog cupboard.

- *Frisbees* If you can find one robust enough, these achieve the maximum distance with the minimum of effort. Accuracy, however, is not always guaranteed,

- *Squeaky toys* Ideal for puppies that are teething, they give them something to chew that isn't human, animal or antique. The squeak can become a little annoying after a few seconds, and turn previously calm, stress-free owners (or neighbours) into psychopathic killers. Manufacturers could easily make squeaky toys that emitted squeaks at frequencies only the dog could hear, but that wouldn't be as much fun.

- *Tug-of-war ropes* Some behaviourists dislike toys that encourage tug-of-war games, because they teach a dog that pulling is acceptable behaviour, which might be fine when what's in the dog's mouth is a rope toy, but not quite so good when it's someone's pet rabbit. There are even rope toys constructed from thousands and thousands of tiny threads, designed to floss between a dog's teeth as they play with it. Occasionally, these threads work loose and become detached from the toy and usually end up flossing the dog's entire internal digestion system before reappearing at the other end.

- *Kongs* Kongs come in various sizes, the largest of which are called, predictably, King Kongs. They are odd grenade-shaped toys made out of thick, heavy-duty rubber and they are often hollow. Their unusual shape means that when thrown in a park, their direction changes with every bounce, keeping a dog on its paws. To keep a dog quiet, but stimulated, the idea is to fill a kong with some treats and let the dog play with it to encourage the treats to fall out. Warning: dogs on a mission to empty a kong take no consideration of their surroundings. If it rolls under the stand for a Ming vase or the 50-inch plasma TV, rest assured that's where the dog is going next, whatever the consequences.

- *Dog-proof toys* There are no such things.

HOLIDAYS

Just like humans feel the need to escape their dreary lives for a few weeks every year, so too do dogs. And for those dogs who are lucky and pampered enough to be taken along, there are certain fundamentals to bear in mind.

Pet Passports

Obviously these are only necessary if you are travelling outside the UK (or Ireland). There is a very good reason for strict regulations about the movement of dogs across international borders. It's called 'rabies', which is a nasty viral infection that targets the brain and nervous system of animals and humans. Once someone starts exhibiting symptoms, the disease is usually fatal. Although the rabies virus can be carried by a variety of mammals, the most common cause of human infection is from dogs. While a bite is the most common form of transmission, the virus can be transferred from dog to human through its saliva. So it's never a good idea to nuzzle a dog that's foaming at the mouth.

The UK is rabies free, mainly because, historically, when any dogs or other pets were brought into the country, they were quarantined for up to six months. This meant keeping them locked up in secure areas, with limited exercise, which many people realise is longer than some humans get for perverting the course of justice. In October 2001, European countries introduced the Pet Travel Scheme, which has become known as the 'Pet Passport', which requires a minimum of three actions:

1. *Microchipping.* Every dog that wants to travel abroad (and return to the UK) must be microchipped for identification purposes. So no passport photo is necessary.

2. *Vaccination.* All booster vaccinations should be up to date, but the dog also needs to be vaccinated against the rabies virus. A dog can't travel for 21 days after its first vaccination, but can travel immediately after any boosters. Non-EU countries require an additional blood test to be carried out 30 days after the vaccination to prove that it has worked.

3. ***Pet Passport.*** This is the documentation that identifies the unique number on the dog's microchip, and also bears confirmation of the dog's rabies vaccination.

The Pet Passport has since been extended to many other countries, offering dogs an opportunity to travel the world with their humans. For some reason, very few dogs are keen on the idea of visiting Korea.

Kennels and Dog Hotels

For some owners, a holiday is as much a break from the dog as it is from work. Instead of going on holiday with their hound, they put them into boarding kennels, where they hope their dog will be looked after, fed and watered. In most cases they are, but it is always a good idea to go on personal recommendation rather than rely on claims of excellence and high standards of care on a website. Kennels also ensure that dogs are exercised and kept clean, fit and healthy. It is frequently tempting to leave the children there.

While kennels might be perceived as the boarding house end of the accommodation scale, owners who prefer their dogs to have a little luxury while they're on holiday, will book pampered pooches into a dog hotel. In a kennel a dog might have its own pen (if it's lucky), in a dog hotel it will have its own room or even a suite. A fresh duvet, Jacuzzi and 24-hour room service might also be advertised, but treat such assurances with scepticism.

Larger kennels can cater for many dogs, whereas hotels have fewer 'guests', enabling staff to devote better one-to-one attention to the dog than a kennel can offer. Of course, should a dog be pampered too much, it might be reluctant to return home. Even if it deigns to do so, don't be surprised if it assumes all sorts of airs and graces and expects you to be at its beck and call. (Some owners might wearily say: 'No change there then.')

BEATING OBSTACLES

Beach Banned
Most dogs love beaches, but they are not always allowed on them. Most local authorities apply by-laws preventing dogs from going on certain beaches between specific times of year. This is to keep beaches, particularly sandy ones, clean and free from dog waste.

As a bluffer, you will know of ways to get around this:

- While a dog can be banned from a beach, it can't be banned from a public footpath, or right of way. Seek out beaches with public rights of way that cross them. A dog is a natural accompaniment and people are legally permitted to wander along a right of way with a natural accompaniment. (A natural accompaniment can also be a pushchair, pram, or motorised scooter.)

- Beach bans apply to the beach. Avoid the beach by carrying the dog down to the sea and swimming in it. If the dog's paws are not touching the beach, then technically, it is not on the beach.

- Only go to beaches between 1 October and 30 April, because this is when most beach bans don't operate.

- Get an alarm clock. Some beach bans only operate from 7am until 10pm, which means you can legitimately take your dog onto a banned beach at any other time.

Fireworks
When Guy Fawkes tried to blow up the Houses of Parliament in 1605, little did he know he would become the bête noire of dogs everywhere.

Because dogs see most things in blue, green or grey, once you've seen one firework, you've seen them all. For our canine friends it's the noise that does the damage. An estimated 40% of dogs are frightened by the noise fireworks make. While recent firework regulations have imposed maximum noise levels for human ears, they've done nothing to protect dog ears. With their superior hearing, even the quietest Catherine wheel assaults their ears mercilessly. The loudest fireworks explode at 120 decibels, which is the equivalent noise level of a jet airplane flying low overhead, or attending a Megadeth concert. Human hearing can be damaged at 85 decibels, which probably explains why many old rock stars are as deaf as posts. Not only can 120-decibel noise be heard, it can also be felt, as the shockwaves pass through our bodies. This can cause distress to a dog during the peak times of the year for firework parties: Bonfire Night, Christmas, New Year, Diwali, Chinese New Year and that moment in the far distant future when the England football team finally wins a penalty shoot-out.

Tips to make these stressful times easier for the dog include:

- Make a safe place for your dog to hide, such as under a bed or table, or behind the sofa.

- Take dogs out for their exercise during daylight hours, when fireworks are less likely to go off.

- At night, close all windows and doors, and draw the curtains to shut out the noise. Put on some gentle, soothing music. Alternatively, play your favourite heavy metal music at just under 120 decibels to drown out the firework noise.

Desensitising Dogs

Stress levels can be reduced by desensitising a dog to the noise and sudden and unexpected bangs that fireworks make. This can involve a trip to the vet and a subsequent deterioration of your finances.

Medication is available to help calm your dog. Always follow the guidelines for the recommended dose. If your dog starts smoking exotic cigarettes, chilling by the pool, and writing bad poetry, an overdose may well have occurred.

Those wishing to avoid going down the medical route might buy a CD instead – ironically, a soundtrack of fireworks going off. *Sounds Scary!* is a collection of firework noises, bangs and whistles that you can download from iTunes. The treatment begins by playing the tracks quietly in the background, and then over the course of several weeks, gradually increasing the volume. If your dog does not know how to use iTunes, burn the tracks onto a CD and let him play them on your hi-fi system.

Pheromone Diffusers

If desensitising your dog doesn't work, then another option to try is DAP – dog appeasing pheromones. This is a synthetic copy of the natural chemical that a dog's mother produces soon after giving birth. It helps to keep a newborn pup calm and reassured, and it can also help to calm older dogs too. These pheromones can be bought in an air-freshener-like dispenser that you plug into a wall socket. Who knows, it might work for you too.

Many employers find dogs to be better workers than their human counterparts. They're not unionised, so they will happily work overtime, and they are unlikely to demand additional remuneration or benefits.

ON THE JOB

There are some dogs who have to earn their living. Many employers find them to be better workers than their human counterparts. Dogs are not unionised, so they will happily work overtime, and they are unlikely to demand additional remuneration or benefits.

Dogs discovered many thousands of years ago that if they made themselves useful they would be more likely to be treated as valuable members of the human family. So in the early days, dogs always had a job to do. Traditionally this was limited to rounding up livestock, helping out with hunting and warning of intruders – but latterly it has extended to assisting in law enforcement, acting as guides for the blind, detecting certain illnesses, and taking part in rescue missions. Mostly, however, dogs have proved most helpful at providing companionship. In return they receive warmth, shelter, food – and a fair amount of love and affection.

SNIFFER DOGS

Well, you can't blame humans for using a dog's best skill. What might be surprising is just how much a sniffer dog can sniff out. Occasionally called 'detection dogs', these animals are trained to detect specific items or substances. While commonly used for detecting illegal drugs, blood, explosives and firearms, dogs have also been used to sniff out bee nests, mobile phones (in prisons), corked wine, and even bedbugs. In America, sniffer dogs are used to detect the quagga mussel, an invasive species sometimes found on the bottom of boats – preferably when they're in dry dock.

At airports, dogs in smart fluorescent tunics hop from suitcase to suitcase sniffing out illegal substances, with an energy level only an animal high on drugs could maintain. Why do you think they're always looking for more?

However, a recent study in Australia demonstrated that some sniffer dogs needed to go back to basic training. New South Wales police dogs dutifully accused over 14,000 people of carrying illegal substances, but after being stopped by the police for further searching, only 3,000 were found to be in possession of anything suspicious. The remaining 11,000 presumably just smelt offensive. In fairness, it should be remembered that a sniffer dog is only as good as its human trainer.

However, in 2005, one British sniffer dog was reported to be so good at her job that she was earning more money than the force's chief constable. Her sense of smell was so keen she could detect traces of blood found on murder weapons that had been scrubbed clean and disinfected. The dog's remarkable expertise meant that she could be hired out to other constabularies for around £500 per day.

SHEEPDOGS

Talk to any sheepdog trainer and they'll tell you that in the sheepdog/sheep farmer relationship, it is the farmer who needs the training, not the dog (although that could be said of any dog/human relationship). Border collies are the most popular breed of sheepdog because of their natural tendency to herd. While some modern farmers claim that a quad bike can do what any sheepdog can do, it should be pointed out that a quad bike does not have a natural herding instinct and it needs a human being to operate it.

Studies have shown that Border collies are capable of identifying more than 250 different objects by name, which is pretty impressive considering they spend all day looking at animals that look exactly the same as each other. Their intelligence was confirmed when in September 2004, a Border collie called 'Striker' went into the Guinness World Records for the fastest car window opening by a dog. It took 11.34 seconds to wind down the window fully, using its paw and nose. That's quicker than a man in a white van.

Perhaps surprisingly, Old English sheepdogs (OES) are less likely to be used for shepherding purposes these days. Their long coats require grooming at least three times a week, making them quite impractical for the fells and mountains. Attempts were made to protect the fur by bringing it together in bunches, but the sheep took one look and refused to be herded by something with pigtails. Traditionally, OES were used by ancient drovers taking cattle to market. These large dogs were ideal for herding larger animals along country tracks. Today, most sheep and cattle reach market in a trailer. This is why Old English sheepdogs took up alternative work, advertising a certain brand of paint.

GUIDE DOGS FOR THE BLIND

Evidence suggests that the blind have been using dogs to help guide them since Roman times. The earliest recorded example of the bond between guide dogs and humans comes from the Roman city of Herculaneum, located close to present day Naples, which was buried along with Pompeii in AD 79 when the volcano Vesuvius erupted. Herculaneum's ruins contain a mural showing a blind figure being unmistakably guided by a dog.

Several attempts were made to train dogs to help blind people in Paris during the late eighteenth century, but it was the First World War that provided the turning point. With so many soldiers blinded by poison gas, a German doctor, Gerhard Stalling, came up with the idea of training dogs in large numbers to help these soldiers. He opened the world's first guide dog school for the blind in 1916. In 1927, an American woman, Dorothy Harrison Eustis, saw the work being done and replicated it in the USA. In 1930, Muriel Crooke and Rosamund Bond set up their own Guide Dog School in the UK. In 1934, the Guide Dogs for the Blind Association was established and has become the world's largest breeder and trainer of working dogs.

Bluffers would do well to remember that these amazing animals are not feted as much as they might be. How many people know that two guide dogs called 'Salty' and 'Roselle' led their blind owners Omar Rivera and Michael Hingson separately down 70 and 78 flights of the World Trade Center shortly before it collapsed in 2001?

HEARING DOGS FOR DEAF PEOPLE

The charity Hearing Dogs for Deaf People was established in 1982, and trains a dog to help a deaf child or adult cope with everyday life. The dogs are taught to react to important noises such as an alarm clock, telephone, doorbell, or smoke alarm and then to attract their owner's attention by nudging them with their nose, or touching them with their paw. The dog then takes the owner to the source of the sound, or a place of safety.

RESCUE DOGS

Whenever there is an emergency, such as a hiker missing on the mountains, an elderly or vulnerable person missing in their local community, or a devastating earthquake, news organisations always refer to the 'rescue dogs' that are called on to help find people. Bluffers will point out that this is actually incorrect terminology. At the risk of sounding pedantic (heaven forbid), the correct description for a rescue dog is actually an 'air-scenting search dog'.

Relying on their powerful sense of smell, an air-scenting search dog is capable of detecting a missing person up to 500 metres away. Together with their human owners, they can be deployed in some of the roughest terrain by 4x4 vehicles, or even lowered by helicopter. Their sensory skills and nimbleness mean that one dog is capable of doing the job of up to 20 human searchers.

The most famous of all rescue dogs is the whisky-barrel-carrying St Bernard. Sadly, the whisky-barrel story is a canine myth. These dogs were sent out in pairs, and when someone was found alive, instead of giving them a nip of whisky to warm themselves, one dog would lie on top of the victim while the other returned to the monks at the monastery near the summit of the Great St Bernard Pass in the Swiss Alps to get further help. With St Bernards weighing anything from 40kg to over 100kg, your chances of survival clearly depended on the lighter of the two dogs lying on top of you.

GUARD DOGS

Dogs have been guarding man since the beginning of their uniquely close relationship. While security firms prefer breeds like Rottweilers, Dobermanns and German shepherds, any dog can be a guard dog. But security men have an image to protect. Apparently it doesn't give quite the right impression if they confront a suspect with a lapdog yapping at the end of a lead.

The role of a guard dog is principally to make a noise to attract a human's attention. If an intruder is not scared by the excessive noise, then further action might be necessitated – in which case the breed of dog comes into play. While all guard dogs should be trained specifically for the job, their natural temperament can influence how they'll deal with intruder:

Basset hound These are placid and affectionate dogs. They dislike being left alone for long periods of time, and so will tend to bark with excitement and look forward to playing games with any intruders.

Border collie If they were given the command, these highly intelligent animals might well be capable of herding an entire criminal gang into a prison cell.

Bulldog Affectionate and loyal, but can be clumsy. Will attack intruders, but just as capable of knocking over a security guard at the same time.

Chihuahua Alert and fearless, they won't let their diminutive six- to eight-inch height get in the way of a good scrap. Unfortunately, they can't scrap much above ankle height.

Dalmatian Outgoing and friendly, these dogs are easily bored. They're likely to fall asleep while the heist is taking place.

Dobermann pinscher Bold and intelligent animals, they love mental stimulation but also make great guard dogs. When not on patrol, they'll be equally happy doing a crossword puzzle.

German shepherd Courageous and love physical exercise. Much prefer being on guard in places where intruders can be chased over high fences, walkways and flat-roofed buildings.

Great Dane Huge, intelligent animals, weighing up to 55kg. They simply bring an intruder down and place a restraining paw on their chest until help arrives.

Labrador retriever Good-tempered and eager to please. High risk of licking intruders to death.

Newfoundland Larger than a Great Dane (up to 68kg), a loveable rogue more interested in water than anything else. Would prefer to go for a swim than chase anyone.

Rottweiler Despite their image, Rottweilers enjoy a cuddle – even if it's with a criminal.

Shih-tzu Affectionate and playful, they can yap as much as any other small dog, however, their coat requires regular grooming. They won't go on guard dog duty if they're not looking perfect.

West Highland terrier Tough and curious, they love getting involved in everything. But they also have a stubborn streak, and if they don't want to go on guard duty then nothing and no one will convince them otherwise.

THERAPY DOGS

Studies have shown that people with pets, such as dogs, have lower blood pressure. But dogs can provide comfort and affection to others, especially the old and infirm. Therapy dogs go into hospitals, hospices, and retirement and nursing homes to provide affection and comfort.

The therapeutic benefits offered by dogs to people first became evident during the Second World War, when a soldier's dog named Smoky was brought into hospital to visit him. Doctors noticed that his spirits lifted as visiting time approached. As time passed, the rest of the ward's patients began looking forward to visiting times too. In the 1970s, an American nurse noticed an improvement in patients when a hospital chaplain brought his dog with him on his visits to the hospital. Now many countries have a Pets As Therapy (PAT) programme or charity. If you claim to know about dogs, you can state with certainty that the bond between two species is never more apparent than in circumstances where people visibly benefit from a dog's company.

KENNEL CLUBS

This a generic term for organisations set up across the world to protect the welfare of dogs. Dog shows became popular during the Victorian period as affluent members of society wanted to show off their purebred animals. However, as these shows became more popular, it was realised that an official body, or organisation, was required to regulate the conduct of dog shows, trials and competitions. There was also a growing need to record stud names and register who began what, when and where. Otherwise any old mutt could bluff its way into the world of purebreds, and that wouldn't do at all.

The Kennel Club, founded in 1873, is the largest organisation in the UK dedicated to the welfare of dogs. Not to be outdone, in 1882 France established the Société

Centrale Canine, while Italy simultaneously founded the Ente Nazionale della Cinofilia Italiana. The American Kennel Club (AKC) was established in 1884, with other societies forming in countries around the world including Australia, India, Canada and South Africa.

While the clubs were established to regulate shows and create a register of pure breeds, they also promote dogs and dog ownership, lobby governments for better dog laws, offer advice to potential dog owners, maintain a list of registered breeders, and run dog training schemes. Somewhere at the heart of all this is a simple and uncomplicated relationship between man and dog, and a good walk.

DOG SHOWS

The first dog show in England was held in 1859 and was designed to raise money for charity. People have been spending small fortunes on backcombing, blow-drying and buffing their dogs ever since. In return there is the tantalising prospect of significant rewards via pedigree stud fees.

The bluffer's position on dog shows should be ambivalent. The best course might be to say that anything that is designed to celebrate the world of dogs is a good thing, as long as their welfare is paramount and their natural dignity is not compromised. Other dog people will nod sagely, and look at you with new respect.

Crufts

Crufts, held annually in the UK, is one of the largest dog shows in the world. The first show took place in 1891 and since then the space required to house the event has been growing at an exponential rate. Today, the Crufts show takes up over 25 acres of exhibition space at Birmingham's NEC. That's a lot of space. That's a lot of dogs. And that's a lot of nappy bags (you will remember why a bluffer will find these preferable to the branded poop-bag version).

The highlight of the show is the judging of each breed, the winners of which go into the 'Best of Breed' category, from which a judge will select, quite literally, the top dog. This entails scrutinising every aspect of the animal, including its coat, body, general health, movement across the floor and even its undercarriage. The very first Best of Breed was won by a greyhound, but the most successful breed of all is the English cocker spaniel, which has won the category seven times. To date, a crossbreed has never been a winner, possibly because they are not allowed to enter. This might explain why a rival show known as 'Scruffts', specifically for crossbreeds of any parentage, is growing in popularity.

Local Country Shows

Whilst Crufts might be the most famous of dog shows, across the world, smaller, local dog shows take place offering any mutt the opportunity to grab a winning rosette. Although local country shows can't offer categories like Best of Breed, what they can offer are more practical competitions, such as 'dog with the waggiest tail', 'dog with the happiest smile', 'dog that most resembles a celebrity', and 'dog that looks most like its owner'. There's even a category for 'dog that has never won anything'.

How many people would still be languishing at the bottom of mine shafts without Lassie?

MEMORABLE MUTTS

Not only have dogs bluffed their way into our households, they've also successfully pawed their way into our entertainment schedules. You can't fail to admire the canine cunning that persuaded mankind to call a popular 30-year-long British TV show containing more sheep than the human population of New Zealand, *One Man and his Dog*. And, just like the real world, our fictional characters have needed a faithful companion at their side. Where would Dr Who have been without his K9? Would Wallace have ever made it to our screens without Gromit? How many people would still be languishing at the bottom of mine shafts without Lassie? And what about all the schoolchildren around the world who might have grown up not knowing that every Shaggy needs a Scooby Doo?

GREYFRIARS BOBBY

The knowledgeable bluffer will recall that John Gray was originally a gardener when he arrived in nineteenth-century Edinburgh, but finding that gardening work during an Edinburgh winter was hard to come by he found himself obliged to look for alternative employment. So 'Auld Jock', as he became known, sought work in the local police force instead.

Paid 13 shillings a week, Auld Jock's beat included the Grassmarket and Greyfriars Kirk areas of Edinburgh, a notorious haunt for criminals at the time. Policemen, or bobbies, were required to have a watchdog, and Auld Jock chose a six-month-old Skye terrier. Then came the duty of naming him and, because he was a police dog, Auld Jock settled on the name 'Bobby', which might not have been terribly original at the time, but came to be synonymous with one of the most famous dogs in history.

Together, Auld Jock and Bobby made a successful team, policing their Edinburgh district for over five years. But in October 1857, Jock developed tuberculosis. As winter progressed, the auld boy deteriorated, and on 8 February 1858 he died at home with Bobby at his feet. Auld Jock was buried in Greyfriars Kirkyard and, despite dogs not being allowed in the graveyard, Bobby was in attendance.

The following day the graveyard's keeper, James Brown, found Bobby lying atop Auld Jock's grave. He chased the dog away, but the next morning he found him lying on the grave again. Brown chased him away once more, but the loyal and determined terrier was back on his master's grave 24 hours later. Eventually Brown took pity on Bobby and allowed him to stay, feeding him from time to time. The graveyard became Bobby's new home, and whatever the weather, he would lie on Auld Jock's grave, something he continued to do until his own death, 14 years later on 14 January 1872. This act of loyalty and devotion has gone down in history, and is now commemorated in Edinburgh with a plaque on Greyfriars Place, a statue (with fountain), and even a pub called Greyfriars Bobby's Bar in Candlemaker Row.

Anybody who aspires to bluff on the subject of dogs and canine behaviour will sniff out a few inconsistencies in this bit of old hokum. 'Cemetery dogs', as they were known, were popular in the late nineteenth century when, in France particularly, people travelled vast distances to feed the dogs they believed were being loyal to their dead masters. Cemetery keepers sometimes brought in dogs to attract such tourists, and if one were to die they would quickly find a replacement. This probably explains why there are differences in the many contemporary purported images of Greyfriars Bobby.

Should you find yourself outside the entrance to Greyfriars Kirk in Edinburgh, remember to pat Bobby's statue, and congratulate him on a good job well done, for he was truly a remarkable dog in many ways. After all, when you know the average life expectancy of a Skye terrier is 12 years, it doesn't take long to do the maths. If Bobby was six months old when Auld Jock acquired him, and then worked as a watchdog for five years, before lying on Auld Jock's grave for a further 14 years, he defied most of the rules regarding his breed's longevity. Ever wondered about the origins of the saying 'Shaggy Dog Story'?

GELERT

When Llywelyn the Great (of Wales) married Joan, daughter of King John of England, one of the King's gifts to the happy couple was a dog called 'Gelert'. Descriptions suggest that Gelert may have been an Irish wolfhound, which is certainly plausible, for these dogs were known for their gentle temperament with children. But they were also capable of seeing off a wolf in a fair fight, and in those days there were quite a lot of wolves around.

One day, when Llywelyn returned from a hunt, Gelert came bounding up to him, his tail wagging, but with blood all around his muzzle. Dashing into his shelter, Llywelyn found his son's crib upturned and the baby nowhere to be seen. Convinced Gelert had killed his son, Llywelyn drew his sword and plunged it into Gelert's body. At the same moment, Llywelyn heard a baby cry and on searching the shelter found his son, safe and well, with the body of a dead wolf nearby. Realising that Gelert had killed the wolf that had threatened his son, he was filled with remorse and buried Gelert in a grand ceremony. Today, people still flock to see Gelert's grave, in the small Welsh village of Beddgelert.

The sceptical bluffer might sniff the telltale signs of yet another load of old hokey, especially when they learn that Gelert's memorial was erected circa 1802 by one David Pritchard, proprietor of the nearby Beddgelert Hotel. Recognising a marketing opportunity when he saw one, Pritchard revived and partly reinvented the story of Gelert and created the grave in an attempt to encourage tourism. His entrepreneurial bent clearly extends beyond his own grave. These days he is reputed to haunt the hotel (now known as the Royal Goat Hotel).

Had Laika not been roaming the streets of 1950s Moscow, she would not have become the first living creature to orbit the earth.

LAIKA

Laika is possibly one of the world's most famous stray dogs, for had she not been roaming the streets of 1950s Moscow, she would not have been picked up and trained to become the first living creature to orbit the earth. The hapless hound was catapulted into the stratosphere some 1,000 miles above the earth, in a cone-shaped vessel which completed one orbit of the earth every one hour and 42 minutes, giving her an average speed of 18,000 miles per hour. She entered orbit on 3 November 1957, causing uproar when it was revealed that there were no plans to bring her back down to earth again. Clearly, the Russians had failed to gauge public opinion. The majority of people weren't too fussy about fellow humans dying in space, but harming dumb animals was a step too far.

Sputnik 2 orbited the earth 2,570 times before falling back to earth on 14 April 1958, burning up on re-entry, by which time Laika was already well and truly dead. While she was the first, she was not the only dog to enter space.

Between 1957 and 1966, the USSR sent 13 dogs into orbit. One dog, Strelka, orbited the earth 18 times (along with a handful of mice, a couple of rats, and some plants) in August 1960 and became the first living creature to return to earth safely. She later went on to give birth to a healthy litter of puppies, one of whom was called 'Fluffy' and given to President John F Kennedy's daughter, Caroline, as a gift by USSR President Nikita Krushchev. Fluffy went on to mate with one of the Kennedy's other dogs, producing a healthy litter of four puppies, which JFK jokingly referred to as 'pupniks'. Dog bluffers really need to know this sort of thing.

PAL

The aforementioned Pal (*see* 'Give a Dog a Bad Name', page 27), became the most famous screen dog in history when he won the coveted role of Lassie. Although he had earlier auditioned for the role, the job was given to a female prize-winning collie, and Pal was taken on as a stunt dog. During a particularly difficult stunt, Pal's performance was so good the film company shot the footage in one take, and decided to award him the main part. The film was a huge success leading to many more films and TV spin-offs.

When Pal retired, the role of Lassie was filled by his direct descendants (of which there were many). There can't be that many film stars who've been able to secure work for the next 10 generations. (Bluffing note: while Lassie was female, Pal and his descendants who played her were exclusively male.)

SHEPTON DASH

Despite being an Old English sheepdog, the paint company Dulux first used this iconic symbol of Englishness in a black-and-white TV Australian advertising campaign in the 1960s. The first Dulux dog was Shepton Dash, who retained the role for eight years before handing the baton on to Fernville Lord Digby, who became such a star that he was collected by a chauffeur and driven to the studios.

Digby was trained by the abrasive TV personality Barbara Woodhouse, and even starred in his own film, *Digby, the Biggest Dog in the World* with Jim Dale and Spike Milligan in 1973. Apart from Shepton Dash, all of Dulux's dogs have been breed champions. Equality arrived in the 1990s when the first female Dulux dog appeared on screen. On set, the dogs were called by their pet names, rather than their official Kennel Club names. In order of appearance, they were Dash, Digby, Duke, Tanya, Pickle and Spud. You never know when this information might come in useful.

HEROIC HOUNDS

It's enough to make you weep, except that bluffers don't weep – nor are they advised to (generally speaking) unless it is clearly to their advantage. On matters of canine heroism however, an exception can be made. You'd have to have a heart of tungsten not to feel a frisson of emotion when you hear another story of a dog entering a dangerously unstable building in a search for survivors, or a dog seriously wounded by shrapnel or bullets still limping on determinedly to disarm the bad guys, or refusing to leave stricken combatants in the field, or carefully leading their blind owners down 70-plus floors of the burning World Trade Center (for which both dogs, Salty and Roselle, won the PDSA Dickin Medal, the world's highest animal honour for gallantry. *See* page 89)

The UK charity PDSA (People's Dispensary for Sick Animals) was founded in 1917 to provide care for sick and injured animals of the poor. It is the country's leading veterinary charity, carrying out more than one million free veterinary consultations a year, and in 1943 it instituted a series of awards to acknowledge outstanding acts of bravery and devotion by animals.

The Dickin Medal, named after the charity's founder Mary Dickin,w is the animal equivalent of the Victoria Cross and has been conferred 70 times, with the greatest number of recipients being dogs (33 at the last count). The winner of the Centenary PDSA Dickin Medal (so-called to mark the charity's 100th birthday in 2017) was Mali, a Belgian Malinois working as a British Military Working Dog on the front line in Afghanistan. On his final deployment he was twice sent through direct fire to detect explosives. He also revealed the precise location of enemy insurgents giving the assault force a vital advantage before engaging in close combat. Mali was seriously wounded by three grenades lobbed at him, causing injuries to his chest, legs and head. Amazingly he survived. Not all the recipients of the award have been so lucky.

In 2015, there was a national outpouring of grief when French police dog Diesel died of multiple gunshot wounds after leading an assault on a suspected terror cell five days after 130 people were killed in Paris.

Both dogs' sacrifices were typical of previous awards made over the past 75 years throughout the world, many of them posthumous.

The bluffer doesn't need a degree in canine psychology to make the following point: dogs feel pain and fear like the rest of us, but if called upon to defend and protect their human companions, they rarely stop to consider the consequences. Not all heroes are people.

'There are moments when verse says infinitely more than a passing remark which teeters on the brink of banality. (Just make sure it isn't doggerel.)'

POOCH POETRY

No other domestic animal, with the possible exception of the horse, has inspired as much poetry as man's best friend. Some of the greatest poets of their age have poured out paeans of love and praise to their canine companions – humbly acknowledging the contribution that their selfless four-legged friends have made to their journey through life.

A line or two of poetry is always helpful at a time when a touching insight into the unique bond between man and dog is appropriate. Bluffers might do well to commit some of the following to memory. There are moments when verse says infinitely more than a passing remark which teeters on the brink of banality. (Just make sure it isn't doggerel.)

The Power of the Dog
(extract)
by Rudyard Kipling

THERE is sorrow enough in the natural way
From men and women to fill our day;
And when we are certain of sorrow in store,
Why do we always arrange for more?
Brothers and sisters, I bid you beware
Of giving your heart to a dog to tear.

Buy a pup and your money will buy
Love unflinching that cannot lie
Perfect passion and worship fed
By a kick in the ribs or a pat on the head.
Nevertheless it is hardly fair
To risk your heart for a dog to tear.

When the fourteen years which Nature permits
Are closing in asthma, or tumour, or fits,
And the vet's unspoken prescription runs
To lethal chambers or loaded guns,
Then you will find - it's your own affair, -
But ... you've given your heart to a dog to tear.

When the body that lived at your single will,
With its whimper of welcome, is stilled (how still!),
When the spirit that answered your every mood
Is gone - wherever it goes - for good,
You will discover how much you care,
And will give your heart to a dog to tear!

Rudyard Kipling (1865–1936) was an English journalist, novelist and poet. Dogs were a constant feature of his life. His most famous work of fiction was arguably *The Jungle Book*, and *If* his most celebrated poem (often described as the nation's favourite), but *The Power of the Dog* is possibly the most famous dog poem of them all. It is a powerful example of a literary work that demonstrates the emotional power dogs can exert over their human family, raising the question about the pain inevitably felt when the dog dies. And yet we continue to enter willingly into this agonising contract. Most erudite dog lovers will be aware of the poem, and will nod both sadly and appreciatively when you allude to it, thus demonstrating your deep understanding of the dog's most famous virtue of unquestioning loyalty and devotion.

To Flush, my dog
(extract)
by Elizabeth Barrett Browning

> *Yet, my pretty sportive friend,*
> *Little is't to such an end*
> *That I praise thy rareness!*
> *Other dogs may be thy peers*
> *Haply in these drooping ears,*
> *And this glossy fairness.*

But of thee it shall be said,
This dog watched beside a bed
Day and night unweary, —
Watched within a curtained room,
Where no sunbeam brake the gloom
Round the sick and dreary.

Roses, gathered for a vase,
In that chamber died apace,
Beam and breeze resigning —
This dog only, waited on,
Knowing that when light is gone,
Love remains for shining.

Elizabeth Barrett Browning (1806–1861) wrote this moving tribute to her cocker spaniel Flush, possibly the most celebrated of all dogs in English literature. Elizabeth had been confined to her sick bed for a long period and Flush had been her inseparable companion during her illness, so much so that the poet credited the dog with human intelligence and an understanding of the written word. Flush featured prominently in the love letters his mistress wrote to her future husband, the writer Robert Browning. A century later the novelist Virginia Woolf wrote the bestselling 'biography' of Flush who entertainingly and insightfully chronicled the celebrated love affair .

An Old Dog Is The Best Dog
By Felix Dennis

An old dog is the best dog,
A dog with rheumy eyes;
An old dog is the best dog
A dog grown sad and wise,
Not one who snaps at bubbles,
Nor one who barks at nowt,
A dog who knows your troubles,
A dog to see you out.

An old bitch is the best bitch,
Not pups to fetch your sticks;
An old bitch is the best bitch,
Not one to teach new tricks,
Not one who's up and leaping,
But one whose coat is grey,
Leg twitching while she's sleeping
In dreams of yesterday.

Felix Dennis (1947–2014) was an English publisher, poet, performer, philanthropist and well-known cynophilist. Bluffers will of course know that aged 23 he gained worldwide notoriety as one of the editors of OZ Magazine, charged with conspiracy to 'deprave and corrupt the morals of the young of the realm'. He was subsequently sentenced to imprisonment until his conviction was quashed on appeal. (At his death he was sole owner of Dennis Publishing leaving an estate worth over £750 million.)

A DOG HAS DIED
(extract)
by Pablo Neruda

> . . . *my dog used to gaze at me,*
> *paying me the attention I need,*
> *the attention required*
> *to make a vain person like me understand*
> *that, being a dog, he was wasting time,*
> *but, with those eyes so much purer than mine,*
> *he'd keep on gazing at me*
> *with a look that reserved for me alone*
> *all his sweet and shaggy life,*
> *always near me, never troubling me,*
> *and asking nothing.*

Pablo Neruda (1904–1973) was a Chilean poet-diplomat and politician who won the Nobel Prize for Literature in 1971. Neruda was described by his contemporary, the better known South American writer Gabriel Garcia Marquez, as 'the greatest poet of the 20th century in any language.' *A Dog Has Died* is one of his best known poems. His is an excellent and unchallengeable name for bluffers to drop into any conversation about dogs in literature.

Geist's Grave
(extract)
By Matthew Arnold

> *But thou, when struck thine hour to go,*
> *On us, who stood despondent by,*
> *A meek last glance of love didst throw,*
> *And humbly lay thee down to die.*
>
> *Yet would we keep thee in our heart—*
> *Would fix our favorite on the scene,*
> *Nor let thee utterly depart*
> *And be as if thou ne'er hadst been.*
>
> *And so there rise these lines of verse*
> *On lips that rarely form them now;*
> *While to each other we rehearse:*
> *Such ways, such arts, such looks hadst thou!*
>
> *We stroke thy broad brown paws again,*
> *We bid thee to thy vacant chair,*
> *We greet thee by the window-pane,*
> *We hear thy scuffle on the stair. . . .*

Matthew Arnold (1822–1888) was a poet and critic and, incidentally, the son of Thomas Arnold the famed headmaster of Rugby School. *Geist's Grave* was written for the poet's four-year-old dachshund, and has a certain elegiac quality. If you're feeling particularly lyrical you might say something like 'in its pathos, waggish affection, and blend of both high seriousness

THE BLUFFER'S GUIDE TO DOGS

and humour, Geist's Grave is one of Arnold's most charming, yet deeply felt, elegies.' To be on the safe side you might add: 'I didn't say that. The Canadian academic W. David Shaw did.'

Of course no review of dog-related verse could be considered complete without reference to Elvis Presley's harrowing song about Old Shep, the dog he grew up with, who rescued him from drowning, but whose eyes were now 'growing dim' and whose time had clearly come. As Elvis heads out to the field with Old Shep, blinded by tears, he raises a gun with trembling hands, and rails at the heavens 'I wish they'd shoot me instead!' Shep looks up at him and rests his old head on his knee. . . . and . . . no, no, Elvis doesn't blow his knee off. All that bluffers need to know is that Old Shep is now in a happier place.*

*Bluffers can console themselves with the knowledge that Elvis never actually had a dog called Shep.

MAN'S (AND WOMAN'S) BEST FRIEND

There is nothing new about the following truisms, but they bear repeating nonetheless.

Dogs are better than men because:

- They don't have problems expressing affection in public.

- They always miss you when you are gone.

- They look at you when you talk to them.

- They don't feel threatened by your intelligence.

- They understand what NO means.

- They never laugh at how you throw the ball to them.

- They don't fall about laughing when they break wind.

- They can't wait to go for a walk with you.

- They understand if some of their friends cannot come inside.

- They think you are a culinary genius.

- They're nice to your relatives.

- They don't demand that you dress in fishnets and high heels.

- They don't care what you look like or how much weight you've gained.

- They don't criticise your friends.

- They don't shout if you take a wrong turn.

- They don't care whether or not you shave your legs.

- They don't feel threatened if you earn more than they do.

- They mean it when they kiss you.

- They don't have a mid-life crisis and abandon you for a younger owner.

- They can be neutered legally.

Dogs are better than women because:

- They don't cry for no reason.

- They love it when your mates come round.

- They don't expect a call when you're late (in fact the later you are the more excited they are to see you).

- They forgive you for playing with other dogs.

- They don't notice if you call them another dog's name.

- They don't mind if you give their offspring away.

- They don't like shopping.

- They like it when you leave your underwear on the floor.

- They never want to talk about their relationship with you.

- They like beer and pubs.

- Their parents never stay for the weekend.

- They don't snap when you refuse to ask for directions.

- They never ask if you think their bum's too big

- They never expect flowers, or complain if you forget their birthday.

- They don't want to know about other dogs you've had.

- They don't believe everything they read in a magazine article.

- They don't take hours to get ready to leave the house.

- They find you fascinating when you're drunk.

- They can't talk.

Dogs don't expect a call when you're late (in fact the later you are the more excited they are to see you).

ß

There's no point in pretending that you know everything about dogs – nobody does – but if you've got this far and you've absorbed at least a modicum of the information and advice contained within these pages, then you will almost certainly know more than 99% of the rest of the human race about what makes dogs tick, how they can be good for us, how they can be bad for us, why our relationship with them is based on an understanding going back many thousands of years, and why the world would be a very different place without them.

What you now do with this information is up to you, but here's a suggestion: be confident about your newfound knowledge, see how far it takes you, but above all have fun using it. You are now a bona fide expert in the art of bluffing about man's oldest friend. Just don't forget that the loveable mutt lying on its back in front of the fire shares more than 98% of its DNA with a wolf.

GLOSSARY

Aversive A type of dog training method involving something a dog doesn't enjoy, like loud noises and electric-shock collars (the latter usually employed by cretins who believe in pain as a way of disciplining dogs).

Bath Useful word to use as warning if a dog is contemplating rolling in some fox poo.

Bed As in 'your' bed. The Holy Grail for all dogs.

Cynophilist Formal name for a dog lover. There is no such word as 'canophile'.

Dewclaw A vestigial digit above the paw pad on the inside of a dog's front legs. Easily torn. Also called 'Dog's thumb'. If a dog is limping the bluffer should check it out first.

Docking A cosmetic procedure whereby a dog's tail

is amputated. Akin to mutilation and illegal in most of Europe. Don't listen to any justification for it; there isn't one.

Dogged Devotion If you use the noun, the adjective is redundant.

Down Frequently used command word for inviting a dog to leave the postman alone.

Dreams There is no cause for alarm when dogs start twitching, yelping, drooling and growling in their sleep. They dream just like humans do.

Give A command to a dog to hand over something of unusual interest it has clamped between its jaws. Like that's going to happen.

Heel A command and position in which a dog walks close to your side. Invariably ignored.

Humping *See* 'Off'.

Kibble Unidentifiable compound that goes into dried dog food. Not particularly appetising.

Korea A useful word to use if the dog is refusing to change his bad-behaviour patterns.

Leave it A command to ignore whatever it is the dog happens to be interested in. This is frequently another dog's stool, which has the remarkable effect of rendering your dog temporarily deaf.

Neutering A means of preventing unwanted pups. Dogs, of either sex, are unlikely to thank you for removing the relevant organs.

Off Word used to tell dog to vacate your favourite chair. Or when a male dog is mounting another dog, a cushion, a large stuffed toy, a tortoise, or anything it's not supposed to. In other words, most objects, inanimate or not.

Pack A group of humans which a dog will imagine it is in charge of. It usually is.

Reward A treat given to a dog for a correct response to an instruction – or to give to a dog anyway because it's looking so loveable.

Ruff The thick fur around a dog's chest, shoulders and neck. Also a joyful noise it makes when it's happy.

Separation anxiety When your dog becomes anxious and stressed when you leave it. Or when joint owners leave each other.

Sit A word common in dealing with dogs, and one which they generally obey if a human is holding something interesting. Also the source of many weak jokes about what a dog might do if it mishears you.

THE BLUFFER'S GUIDE TO DOGS

White dog stools Mysterious phenomenon which characterised the colour of all dog excrement until the mid-1980s, when it just as mysteriously disappeared. A bluffer will say that it could have something to do with the reduced calcium in dogs' diets.

A BIT MORE BLUFFING...

Bluffer's® GUIDE TO BREXIT

Bluffer's® GUIDE TO CRICKET

Bluffer's® GUIDE TO MANAGEMENT

Bluffer's® GUIDE TO CYCLING

Bluffer's® GUIDE TO SOCIAL MEDIA

Bluffer's® GUIDE TO ETIQUETTE

Bluffer's® GUIDE TO RACING

Bluffer's® GUIDE TO GOLF

Bluffer's® GUIDE TO WINE

Bluffer's® GUIDE TO JAZZ

Bluffer's® GUIDE TO DOGS

Bluffer's® GUIDE TO FISHING

Bluffer's® GUIDE TO OPERA

Bluffer's® GUIDE TO CHOCOLATE

Bluffer's® GUIDE TO CATS

Bluffer's® GUIDE TO BEER

Available from all good bookshops

bluffers.com